JUST LIKE US

Just Like Us

STEF LISTON

survivor

First published 2008

Cover design by Mark Prentice

ISBN 978 1 842913 57 4

Survivor is an imprint of
KINGSWAY COMMUNICATIONS LTD
26–28 Lottbridge Drove, Eastbourne BN23 6NT, UK
info@survivor.co.uk

Printed in Great Britain

Contents

One of Those Moments

It was one of those moments. It was quite unexpected and the field opposite the house triggered it. It was Christmas night, 2003, and we'd been enjoying the day at my mum's house in Kent. I'd gone outside to get something from the car, and that's when it happened. A quick glance at the field, now too dark even to make anything out, and 'Bang!' – it happened. The moment went, almost as soon as it had come, but its impact was real. It was like being invited in to something too big to work out. It *was* just a feeling, but I think God was in it; maybe it was what the Bible describes as 'deep calling to deep' (Psalm 42:7 NASB).

Let me explain about the field. It sits opposite the front door of my mum's house and it's just an ordinary field – you probably know the kind, grass, etc., but when I became a Christian, aged 18, it became 'sacred ground', my place of prayer. And here I was, over 12 years later, a 30-year-old husband and daddy of two, being beckoned by God into a deeper friendship with Him. What triggered it was the sight of that field, the place where I'd poured my heart out to God, where I'd got to know Him and let Him get to know me. It was the spot where I'd encountered God, and I was thrilled as this fresh invitation gripped me.

I thought the family might not appreciate it if I disappeared into the field there and then, but the experience and sense of invitation has stayed with me, fuelling the fire inside – calling me to an exploration further into the depths of God.

That's what this book is about – explorations into God. It's called *Just Like Us* because Elijah, that great hero of God, is described in the book of James (5:17 NIV) as a man 'just like us'. Throughout this book we will look at different heroes who were just like us, see what they learned in prayer, and learn from them.

This book doesn't cover everything there is on prayer. No. It's a book which tries to communicate how our effectiveness in prayer, our 'spiritual muscle', is interwoven with our intimacy with God. I hope it gets you in the guts and draws you deeper. If it manages this, I'll be a happy man.

Let me just say that when it comes to the Bible readings early on in each chapter, do me a favour and make sure you read them properly. Don't be lazy! Read them and read them slowly, otherwise you'll be guessing your way through each chapter and not growing in knowledge of the actual Bible. Thanks.

Here we go, then.

It's Not What It Was

During the chapters that follow, you'll notice a lot of 'fighting talk' and some nasty situations. You may find yourself feeling a bit overwhelmed and thrown in at the deep end.

The thing is, we find ourselves living in a world which has fallen from what it once was, into what it now is. And what it once was is *very* different from what it now is. When God originally created the earth, it was all 'very good' (Genesis 1:31), and although it's still amazing and full of God's glory, it has, at the same time, been ruined by sin. Crazy things happen, and sometimes it can *appear* that the devil's got a free rein.

Our world needs warriors. When Adam was originally created, it seems that walking in the garden with God was about as strenuous as things got! When sin entered the world, there was a change in the state of play, and suddenly things were going to get a bit tougher (see Genesis 3:14–19).

I don't like hardship for the sake of hardship (who does?), and I wouldn't choose to fight if peace was an option. But facts are facts. Until Jesus returns and God makes everything new, our current world is a battleground and not a playground. Ignore that truth at your own peril.

Because of this, I make no bones about the fact that in writing this book I'm endeavouring to prepare you to fight well, and to come through whatever is thrown at you, victoriously.

There was a time, in the beautiful Eden garden, where sin wasn't even known about. Adam and Eve would have enjoyed themselves and one another and God in friendships unspoilt by misunderstanding, fear or guilt. One day all that will be restored, and a whole lot more besides. The glory of that day is beyond imagination, and if you're in Christ, you're going to be there. That day will usher in an eternity of peace, joy and abundant life, completely untouched by sin and its dire consequences.

In the meantime, we find ourselves sandwiched between what was and what will be. It's an age of pressure, trial and warfare. What's required is courage, patience and a pure heart. God is very keen to equip us to meet the challenges with joy and a light heart. I pray that He uses this book to that end.

1

Jacob Wrestles with God

Setting the scene

It's true that God chose Jacob and loved him, but here's the honest truth: he was one slippery character! You wouldn't trust him as far as you could throw him.

Someone who knew first-hand about him was his twin brother, Esau. From the day they were born there was friction between them, and there couldn't have been more opposite twin brothers. Esau was all covered in hair, and Jacob had that 'just-waxed' look; Esau was an expert hunter, and Jacob liked to stay indoors cooking. Neither of them was particularly godly, but for some unknown reason God had especially chosen to bless Jacob (see Romans 9:10–13).

Jacob made his way in life through trickery and deceit, and twice Esau (a bit of a wally as well as an expert hunter) was the victim of his schemes. As a result, Esau was obviously bent on revenge and so Jacob had to run. He fled to his uncle Laban's, where he stayed for 14 years, during which time he married both his uncle's daughters, as well as gathering heaps of possessions and animals.

After the 14 years, things had got a bit tense with Laban regarding sheep and business, so Jacob decided to pack up and leave, returning home.

On the way back, a very strange thing happened. They arrived at a stream called the Jabbok, and Jacob sent all of his family and possessions over to the other side, while he remained.

Jacob . . . spent the rest of the night alone.

A man came and fought with Jacob until just before daybreak. When the man saw that he could not win, he struck Jacob on the hip and threw it out of joint. They kept on wrestling until the man said, 'Let go of me! It's almost daylight.'

'You can't go until you bless me,' Jacob replied.

Then the man asked, 'What is your name?'

'Jacob,' he answered.

The man said, 'Your name will no longer be Jacob. You have wrestled with God and with men, and you have won. That's why your name will be Israel.'

Jacob said, 'Now tell me your name.'

'Don't you know who I am?' he asked. And he blessed Jacob.

Jacob said, 'I have seen God face to face, and I am still alive.' So he named the place Peniel [in Hebrew 'Peniel' means 'face of God']. The sun was coming up as Jacob was leaving Peniel. He was limping because he had been struck on the hip, and the muscle on his hip joint had been injured.

(Genesis 32:24–32)

Insights

Strange story? Yes. Things to learn from it? Yes again.

The first thing to notice is that before the fight took place,

Jacob was left alone. It seems that Jacob knew it had to be this way, as you watch him sending even his closest family over to the other side of the river away from him. He probably didn't realise exactly what was going to happen, *but he knew he had to be alone with the Lord.*

There's something about our intimacy with the Lord which highlights the true measure of our strength. Let me explain. Sometimes we get carried along by the spiritual gusto of pastors and friends, which is OK now and then, but a dangerous full-time hobby. Reality hits when those people are no longer around and we discover (to our horror) that there's no real substance between ourselves and God. All the Christian meetings and conferences in the world won't do if you're not regularly getting up close and personal with God Himself. I love hanging out in big crowds with my wife, but if that was all I did, our marriage would suffer; we need those regular one-on-one moments as well. It's the same with us and the Lord.

Back to the fight. It can't be denied that this was one serious struggle. I dread to think just how hard it was. I attend a boxing club once a week, and we train and spar for three-minute sessions and then have a one-minute break, and there are times when it's pure torture; my arms feel like lead, my will faints within me, the three-minute rounds seem more like three hours, and there's no way our break lasts a full minute! *Strange things happen when you're hurting.* You begin to question just how much you really want what you came for, and what price you're willing to pay for it. The true measure of your desire is tested.

But look at Jacob. There may have been a lot of things about him that were rotten, but he had learned a thing or two in the past 14 years. *He knew he needed the blessing of God*

– not a stolen blessing, not a deceitful blessing, but God's blessing, received directly from Him in prayer.

This raises the question: if Jacob had to fight so hard, did the Lord actually *want* to bless him? Of course He did, otherwise there's no way any of this would have happened. Remember, it's not Jacob who picks the fight with God, but God who picks the fight with Jacob. Why? So that Jacob would wrestle with Him and get a blessing!

There are times when what I can only describe as a 'fight' wells up in our spirit, when we're so dissatisfied with the situation and so desperate to see God move that we find a lonely place and wrestle with Him for His favour and blessing to be poured out. Where does that 'fight' come from? It's the Holy Spirit within us, initiating a wrestling match, so that we can lay hold of God for what is actually His will (see Philippians 3:12).

But even with this in mind, there are moments in the scrap when it seems that God actually doesn't want to bless you (as we saw the angel say to Jacob, 'Let go of me! It's almost daylight'). But this isn't true! God wants to develop in you such a hunger for His blessing, and such a confidence in His promises to bless and save and heal and transform, that you say, 'You can't go until You bless me.' This is the prayer that prevails. It's not always easy, and it can be lonely; it's not always instant, and it can be painful – but it's worth it.

This story is about desire. Just how much did Jacob want God's blessing? How much do you want it? Do you want it enough to fight for it?

Finally, there were two things that changed about Jacob as a result of this incident; two marks of God's blessing.

The first was a name change. Jacob means 'supplanter',

which basically means that he couldn't be trusted and would do all he could to take what was yours and keep it for himself. His name was changed to Israel, which means 'to struggle with God'. What sort of name change is that? Well, it seems that instead of being a slippery, two-faced character, treading on others to get ahead, he had become a man who lived plainly and honestly before others and brought his interests before God alone. He was to become someone who, before he went anywhere else and started making plans, would come to God and thrash things out with Him, and find *His* will for his life.

The second change was the dislocated hip. Jacob, or should I say Israel, would never be able to forget this turning point in his life. He had been undone on a human level; he was no longer the self-made man, independent and self-sufficient. He had become God's man. He walked with a limp because he was permanently injured. God won't think twice about injuring your ego. You might well learn to prevail in prayer with God, but in the process He will make you realise your weakness and frailty, so that you learn to look to Him and Him alone. There's a cost to walking with God. You might look a bit funny like Israel, limping along, but you'll be a lot better for it.

The result

Jacob meets his brother Esau, who wanted to kill him, and they end up cuddling! God seems to soften Esau's heart and Jacob is able to live in harmony with him.

Conclusion

Jacob was willing to be alone with God, without depending on others, and to wrestle with Him *through the night* in order to get the necessary blessing from God. Jacob wouldn't let go of God until he had received his heart's desire from Him. The result of the struggle was a new name, which meant a new identity, and an injury, which spoke of his weakness and God's power. Jacob fought with God, and prevailed.

Ask yourself

- Are you willing to go the long haul, and keep holding on to God when you feel as though you've got nothing left?
- Are you willing to trade in your ego and self-esteem in exchange for an intimate walk with God?

2

Moses Changes God's Mind

Setting the scene

Picture this: Moses has been up on Mount Sinai in the wilderness for 40 days and 40 nights, receiving specific instructions from God for the recently rescued Israelites. It's an awesome sight to behold, as the top of the mountain is covered with the glory of the Lord (see Exodus 24:12–18). The Israelites didn't want to meet God because His glory was too terrifying (thunder, lightning, angelic trumpets, mountain shaking, etc.), so they were more than happy for Moses to be up the mountain on their behalf. They were happy, that is, until he didn't come back when they expected him to. They probably thought he would be a day or two, maybe even a week, but when it took longer than a few weeks they began to grumble.

So what do they do? Send someone up after Moses? No way. They turn to Plan B – make another god! Get some gold, mould it into the shape of a calf and then say to the people, 'This is your God, who rescued you from Egypt.' So they do this and then have an orgy to celebrate. Let's pick up the story there. . .

> The LORD said to Moses: 'Hurry back down! Those people you led out of Egypt are acting like fools. They have already stopped obeying me and have made themselves an idol in the shape of a young bull. They have bowed down to it, offered sacrifices, and said that it is the god who brought them out of Egypt. Moses, I have seen how stubborn these people are, and I'm angry enough to destroy them, so don't try to stop me. But I will make your descendants into a great nation.'
>
> Moses tried to get the LORD God to change his mind: 'Our LORD, you used your mighty power to bring these people out of Egypt. Now don't become angry and destroy them. If you do, the Egyptians will say that you brought your people out here into the mountains just to get rid of them. Please don't be angry with your people. Don't destroy them! Remember the solemn promise you made to Abraham, Isaac and Jacob. You promised that some day they would have as many descendants as there are stars in the sky and that you would give them land.'
>
> So even though the LORD had threatened to destroy the people, he changed his mind and let them live.
> (Exodus 32:7–13)

Insights

Before we get into details, notice three things. First, God's people are sometimes silly – belonging to Him doesn't automatically mean that you get it right. Second, our stupidity affects God – when we sin because we don't trust Him, God is grieved and that is serious. Third, one man living right before God can make a massive difference.

This chapter is about intercession, which is a certain type of prayer. The dictionary defines intercession as 'the action of pleading with somebody in authority on behalf of somebody else, especially somebody who is to be punished for something'. It's a perfect description of this story. Moses is the intercessor, God is the One in authority, and the Israelites are the people about to be punished.

Now I don't know about you, but if God had said to me what He said to Moses, I don't think I would have argued! God explicitly says, 'Don't try to stop me.' So what does Moses do? He tries to stop Him. What's the deal here? Why did Moses try to stop God and, more importantly, *why did it work*?

The answer lies in two 'things-you-must-know-if-you-want-to-intercede-effectively'. First, you've got to know what God is like, and second, you've got to know what God has promised. Moses takes his stand on those two facts.

So what is God like? Well, Moses knew that God's dramatic rescue of the Israelites was about demonstrating His power and glory (see Exodus 7:1–5). God loves doing this, because when His glory is seen, His people rejoice and celebrate at what an amazing God they have, and His enemies quake and go into hiding – perfect!

So Moses argues that if God destroys the Israelites, the Egyptians will cuss Him, saying He couldn't finish what He started. Imagine that! Those arrogant Egyptians, who had been so humbled by God's power, would lift up their heads again and mock the living God. Moses knows that the most important thing to God is His reputation, and so he uses this in intercession.

But Moses doesn't stop there. He also reminds God that He

has already *promised* Abraham, Isaac and Jacob centuries before that their descendants (the Israelites) would be numbered in millions and given a land by Him (the place they were on their way to). This promise is found in Genesis 12:1–3. If God destroyed them, He would be going back on His promise. Unthinkable! So Moses knows the promises of God, and uses them in intercession.

Check this: *God responds by changing His mind*. Ignore these two prayer-treasures at your own expense.

It's vital to notice that Moses *doesn't* say, 'But God, how can You destroy the people? All the hard work and pain *I've* put into these people for You, and the only thanks *I* get is this! Spare a thought for *me* here! Are You telling me *I* did all this for nothing?' Moses doesn't do that, because he knows that at the end of the day, he's just a servant anyway; it's only right that he serves God, so he can't rightly complain. Selfish, sulky behaviour doesn't shake the heavens; God is so much bigger than that and so should we be. In fact, where God puts the focus onto Moses, Moses actually puts it back onto God. God says, 'Those people *you* led out of Egypt are acting like fools.' Moses says to God, 'Our Lord, *You* used *Your* mighty power to bring these people out of Egypt.' With all reverence, Moses refuses to carry God's burden or own God's property. This is true humility and draws out a power-buster from God (a power-buster is a premiership-level answer to prayer, in case you were wondering), who decides to have mercy on the people.

This can seem confusing, because in this story God can look indecisive, or even mistaken. Some people side-step this by saying that God didn't *actually* change His mind, and that it was all just a test for Moses to see how he would respond.

This would be fine, but the passage makes it clear that God *did* change His mind (verse 13)!

So what's the deal? Does God know the end from the beginning? Yes. Was God taken by surprise in this story? No. Was God in charge of the whole process? Of course; the total sovereignty of God is never undermined by these situations. So what, then? This story helps us not to develop a *wrong view* of God's sovereignty, one where *we* have no real part to play in the story and end up lying in bed all day waiting for God to get us up!

It's mysterious, and we're not sure how it *all* works together, but what the Bible demonstrates beautifully is that God's sovereignty does not exclude our genuine involvement and initiative, and our genuine involvement and initiative does not undermine, threaten or subtract from God's sovereignty. Amen to that!

Interceding effectively involves knowing God's character: that He would much rather show mercy than judgement, and would much rather be known as mighty than weak. Interceding effectively also involves knowing and using God's promises. A promise is like a sword – a beautiful weapon, but not much use until you use it. Use the Scriptures! If all you do with the Bible is read it, then you might as well have a sword for no other reason than to polish it. For the perfect example of swift and deadly swordsmanship, read Matthew 4:1–11.

Christian, don't let the promises we've been given sit around gathering dust. Wield them before God in heaven, until we inherit them on earth.

To stand on these promises before God with unwavering confidence is a dynamic and life-changing experience. Come on now: let's fight.

Finally, don't say that you alone couldn't make a difference. God is always looking for people (John 4:23; 2 Chronicles 16:9) and, as we see in this story, one is enough. It's not that one is ideal, but it *is* enough. If you find yourself alone in a sea of sin and compromise, take your place of intercession and watch what God does.

The result

Because of Moses' intercession, the people are spared. The end result is not ideal, with that generation dying in the wilderness due to their persistent unbelief. Importantly though, God's character is upheld and His promise is fulfilled; and though it's the next generation, the descendants of Abraham, Isaac and Jacob do end up inheriting the land (see the book of Joshua).

Conclusion

In the face of what *seems* to be a decision that's been made by God, Moses takes a confident stand in the other direction based on what he knows of God's unchanging nature. He calls on God to overturn His decision based on what he knows of His character and promises. Moses pleads with God to hold back the anger and pour out the mercy. Moses' example illustrates the vital importance of knowing the character and promises of God, and being willing to stand on them when the pressure's on.

Ask yourself

- Will you stand firm and intercede, based on what you know about the character and the promises of God?

3

Gideon's Not Afraid to Ask

Setting the scene

At this point the Jews had been in the Promised Land for about 120 years, but things weren't going well. In fact, as soon as the generation of Jews who had conquered the land died out, there arose a generation 'who did not know the LORD' (Judges 2:10). These people married foreign people who worshipped foreign gods, and the result was always the same – pick'n'mix religion, a bit of your god and a bit of mine. The result was that God judged them in His anger. God actually strengthened foreign armies so that they would overpower His own people, as discipline for their sin.

In Gideon's time, the Midianites were the bad boys oppressing the Jews; they would invade the Promised Land at harvest time and steal all the food for themselves. It had got to the point where the Jews were so scared they were living in the caves!

Gideon was the youngest member of the weakest family of

one of the smallest tribes, but God had His eye on him, and appeared to him while he was working undercover on a secret stash of wheat. God tells Gideon that He's with him and that He will rescue the people of Israel from their enemies.

Just to say, although Gideon is talking with an angel, I'm including his statement as a prayer because this was no ordinary angel (if there is such a thing!), but the Angel of the Lord. He's a very mysterious Old Testament figure, often equated with the Lord Himself (see Judges 6:12, 14, 16).

> *The angel appeared and spoke to Gideon, 'The LORD is helping you, and you are a strong warrior.'*
>
> *Gideon answered, 'Please don't take this wrong, but if the LORD is helping us, then why have all these awful things happened? We've heard how the LORD performed miracles and rescued our ancestors from Egypt. But those things happened long ago. Now the LORD has abandoned us to the Midianites.'*
>
> *Then the LORD himself said, 'Gideon, you will be strong, because I am giving you the power to rescue Israel from the Midianites.'*
>
> *Gideon replied, 'But how can I rescue Israel? My clan is the weakest one in Manasseh, and everyone else in my family is more important than I am.'*
>
> *'Gideon,' the LORD answered, 'you can rescue Israel because I am going to help you! Defeating the Midianites will be as easy as beating up one man.'*
>
> *(Judges 6:12–16)*

Insights

After Gideon has been told that the Lord is with him, the New American Standard Bible puts Gideon's response like this: 'Oh my lord, if the Lord is with us, why then has all this happened to us? And where are all His miracles which our fathers told us about?' (Judges 6:13 NASB).

There are different kinds of prayer, and this kind of prayer is what you might call 'enquiry'. God brings a message to Gideon through His angel, and Gideon just can't see how it's true, so instead of saying 'OK' without really taking it seriously (ever done that before?), he asks a question in order to find out more.

It's OK to ask God questions. I say this because some Christians seem to think it's rude. Enquiry is important, because sometimes the things God says seem so incredible that not to ask any questions would probably mean we haven't taken Him seriously.

Consider the Virgin Mary, for example. An angel appears and says that not only is she, as a virgin, going to give birth, but her baby will be the Son of God. The first thing she says is, 'How can this be, since I am a virgin?' Fair question! She's not questioning whether or not it will happen, she just has understandable concerns about *how*! Gideon's the same. He doesn't dismiss the heavenly visitor, but asks two excellent questions.

The first one is, *'Why has all this happened to us?'* Gideon realises that it was never God's plan to have His people oppressed and beaten by the enemy. Gideon equates God with victory – and so he should! Sometimes we can get into a fatalistic mindset where we assume everything awful that happens is God's will for us and so we just accept it. This is not good. When things go bad, you need to go to God and ask Him why, because it could be for any number of reasons and the only One with the answer is, of course, God. It could be that, like Israel, you've been rebellious and so God is disciplining you; in which case you need to know, so you can repent and so God can let up. Or it could be that Satan has asked God if he can have a special go at you, as he did with Job (Job 1:9–11; 2:4–5) and Simon Peter (Luke 22:31), and that God (knowing you can handle it) has given him permission. If that's the case, you need to know, so that you can stand your ground and not lose heart. There are other possible reasons, but I've highlighted those two deliberately; in the first instance you're at fault and need to change, but in the second you're not, and it's vital that you're not in the dark about that. Do you see the importance of asking questions?

The second question Gideon asks is, *'Where are all His miracles?'* This is wonderful. The Israelites, like most people of their time, recalled history by storytelling, and their stories were mostly about what God had done in rescuing them from Egypt. Gideon would have been very familiar with all that had happened there, and he seems to have been wondering, 'If the Lord is the same God who did all this, and if He *is* with us, then where are the accompanying miracles?' *He isn't willing to skate over the powerlessness they're experiencing, or the lack of signs and wonders. He won't pretend that it's OK.* If God miraculously delivered the Israelites from a force as mighty as Egypt, and made sure they were provided with gold, silver and all kinds of things, why was Gideon secretly having to beat out some wheat in a wine press? This is an issue of expectation. *To have high expectations of God is to have a high opinion of God, and to have low expectations of God is to have a low opinion of God.* God doesn't need people to make excuses for what He's not doing. He's looking for people who won't listen to excuses. He's looking for a church that will dare to ask Him questions and enquire why His glory isn't being made known as it has been in times gone by. He wants to hear us cry with Gideon, 'Where are the miracles?' If we don't need miracles, then we might as well stop pretending that we want to see His church built and His kingdom grow, because *something supernatural cannot and will not be built by mere natural power*.

The final thing about Gideon seems a little bit tricky. He says that the Lord has abandoned the Israelites. The reason why I've called it tricky is that it implies that God has been unfaithful, which is certainly not the case. The truth is that God had removed His presence from view, not to desert them, but to bring them to the end of their wickedness and draw them back to Himself. The reason why I'm commending Gideon here is that he isn't afraid to pour his heart out to God. There's this reality with him. As far as he's concerned, God has abandoned the Israelites; the Land of Promise is being overrun, and there seems to be no evidence of the benefits associated with knowing God. Gideon isn't saying that God's at fault; he just can't make sense of the situation. There are times when what we read in God's word or hear through prophecy doesn't tally with our experience. When this happens, the first thing to do is to find out if that's what the scripture or prophecy is really saying, or whether you've misunderstood. Once you've settled what has been meant, you then have a responsibility to work it through with God, in all honesty and openness, until your experience matches up; and this doesn't always happen overnight! This might mean you being reverently blunt with God, and asking Him some tough questions. That's OK.

I remember having an argument with my wife on one occasion. It was all a bit tense and there seemed to be no way through on a particular issue. I remember standing in my kitchen and looking out of the window, and just wondering, 'What's this about?' It was an attitude of enquiry. Nothing was working and I needed a revelation from the Lord. Suddenly, out of the blue, I understood what this was about. I went straight back into the front room and asked her a question, which totally unlocked the whole thing. Praise God! It's only a small thing, but it illustrates the fact that God knows the roots, causes and solutions to all difficult situations. As we enquire, and wait, He reveals.

The result

God confirms to Gideon that He's serious about using him, and so Gideon responds obediently and prepares to smash the Midianites. Through a strange process of elimination, God whittles Gideon's army down from 22,000 to 300. God wants a small army just so Israel know that the victory is from God and not by their own power; He wants to show Himself miraculous! This tiny army destroys the Midianites who are too many to number, a mighty victory is won and the Promised Land is restored. Not bad.

Conclusion

Gideon was willing to enquire of God. This demonstrated that he was taking God's message seriously. Gideon expected that if God was truly with him, there would be victory over their enemies as well as miracles. Gideon, though reverent, was blunt with God, because he didn't want to be a pretender.

Ask yourself

• If you're experiencing difficulties, will you come to God and ask Him why, instead of assuming it's just His will?

4

Hannah Gets Desperate

Setting the scene

Family life can sometimes be very complicated – one episode of *EastEnders* bears witness to that! This story describes a desperate family situation. Hannah was the wife of a man called Elkanah and, try as they might, she couldn't get pregnant. In those days and in that culture it wasn't unusual for a man to have more than one wife and Elkanah's other wife – Peninnah – had loads of children. Back then, if a woman couldn't conceive, it was a disgrace, and to make matters worse, Peninnah ribbed Hannah because of it. Although Elkanah tried to make it up to her in other ways, Hannah was a broken woman.

Year after year Elkanah travelled with his family to Shiloh for a holy festival, and year after year Peninnah provoked Hannah so much that she couldn't eat a thing; all she could do was cry. One year she got so desperate that through her tears she promised God that if He would give her a son, she would give him completely to the Lord, to be brought up in the temple.

One day, Elkanah was there [at the temple] offering a sacrifice, when Hannah began crying and refused to eat. So Elkanah asked, 'Hannah, why are you crying? Why won't you eat? Why do you feel so bad? Don't I mean more to you than ten sons?'

When the sacrifice had been offered, and they had eaten the meal, Hannah got up and went to pray. Eli [the priest] was sitting in his chair near the door to the place of worship. Hannah was brokenhearted and was crying as she prayed, 'LORD All-Powerful, I am your servant, but I am so miserable! Please let me have a son. I will give him to you for as long as he lives, and his hair will never be cut.'

Hannah prayed silently to the LORD for a long time. But her lips were moving, and Eli thought she was drunk. 'How long are you going to stay drunk?' he asked. 'Sober up!'

'Sir, please don't think I'm no good!' Hannah answered. 'I'm not drunk, and I haven't been drinking. But I do feel miserable and terribly upset. I've been praying all this time, telling the LORD about my problems.'

Eli replied, 'You may go home now and stop worrying. I'm sure the God of Israel will answer your prayer.'

'Sir, thank you for being so kind to me,' Hannah said. Then she left, and after eating something, she felt much better.
(1 Samuel 1:7–18)

Insights

Put yourself in Hannah's shoes. Not only can she not have children, she also has to share her husband with another woman who can (and is popping them out like there's no tomorrow), and it's not even as if this other woman is nice about it! For Hannah, life's tough and there's no way out. Have you ever felt like that?

When we find ourselves in these kinds of situations, when nothing seems to be going right, it's the easiest thing in the world to back off from God. Our minds can start playing tricks; we can think that God is angry with us or that He doesn't like us any more, or that He's not bothered by our suffering. If we listen to any one of those thoughts, then we'll back off.

This is where Hannah stands out. Somehow, through it all, she knows that God is good and so she doesn't block Him out; instead she comes near to Him and shares her pain with Him.

She's desperate, but you know what? *God loves a desperate soul*. She uses her desperation as fuel for her prayers. Her prayers probably weren't fancy, just a few words mixed with a lot of sobbing and groaning, but God doesn't mind. If you're genuinely pursuing God for the best, there will be times in your life when God will order things in such a way as to make you desperate. He will bring you to a place where you feel hemmed in on every side and what you do at that point will have massive repercussions for your future. Remember Moses when he was leading the Israelites out of Egypt? The Egyptian army takes up the chase and suddenly the Israelites are caught between the army and the sea. A demonic disaster? No! A divine demonstration! As Moses maintains his trust in God and steps out in faith, perhaps the most famous miracle of history takes place as the sea makes way for God's people (see Exodus 14).

Likewise, Hannah maintains her trust in God; she comes near to Him and doesn't allow the pain to drive a wedge between her and the Lord. Hers is an example to be followed. No matter how confused, disappointed or sad you are, let your difficulties be an opportunity for you to put your roots down even deeper into Jesus. Don't let the situation rob you of your pure heart and love for God. These things are too precious to lose, no matter how tough things are.

Another thing that's worth noting is that Hannah's story, although covered in a few lines of your Bible, actually took years from beginning to end. If ever there was an important lesson to learn, it's this: 'for the Lord one day is the same as a thousand years, and a thousand years is the same as one day' (2 Peter 3:8). It's easy to say that, and it sounds very poetic, but it can be painful to live with. What exactly is it getting at?

The first part means that a single day in your life is very important to God and during that day He can make changes in you or do things through you that are so amazing they should really have taken a thousand years.

The second part means that when things seem to be taking forever to happen and you think God isn't hearing you, actually it's only been a few minutes as far as He's concerned, so it would be crazy to give up. As I write, my wife and I are seeking God for something that has been dragging on for years, and you know what? The heavens are silent. Not a dicky bird! It's horrible sometimes, but I know that as far as God is concerned, it hasn't really been going on for that long, and His perspective counts far more than mine, so what can we do? Keep going.

A massive hurdle for Christians is this thing called 'time'. We're told through adverts and posters that we have the right to get whatever we want right now. If we haven't got the money, then get it on credit. Forget the issue of whether or not it's moral to live a lifestyle of debt (Romans 13:8) – if you want it, get it. This way of thinking causes big problems, especially when it comes to inheriting God's promises.

Normally, the promises aren't fulfilled overnight; in fact, they can take years, which can be surprising and disheartening. Let's learn from Hannah. She feels the pain of waiting, but she continues to ask God to work a miracle for her. In fact, with Hannah, the delay increased the devotion! When she was first married she probably just assumed she would have children instantly, but as the years dragged on, she realised this wasn't just going to happen – she needed a miracle. But look at her heart! She's so soft that in the end she tells God that if He will give her a son, she won't keep him for herself. Staggering. This is the fruit of waiting for God.

There's one last thing about Hannah that's worth thinking about. Yes, she was desperate. Yes, she was determined. Yes, she was patient. But in it all, she didn't hide her pain from God. She was honest before Him and honest with herself. As a Christian, it's important not to pretend. There's no point faking it before God, because He searches right into our heart of hearts and knows us inside out. Because of this, why bother putting on a show to ourselves or others?

If you read through the Psalms, you'll probably notice two main things. First, the psalmist is amazed with God, and second, he doesn't hide his feelings from God. In a single psalm you'll often find terrible sadness, tears and confusion coupled with praise and strong confidence in God, and those two sets of feelings *can* go together! The one doesn't cancel out the other (see Psalms 6, 42, 51, 69 and 73 as examples of this).

A great thing about God is that He doesn't mind that we're human. In fact, He made us that way! The Bible says that He actually thinks it's good that we're so frail in ourselves, because when we do amazing things for Him, He gets the glory instead of us (2 Corinthians 4:7). This means that you can share your weaknesses with Him without fear of being dismissed or disqualified. If you can get this, and live in the good of it, I guarantee less stress and a closer walk with God. I make every effort to be brutally honest with the Lord. It sometimes feels a bit strange, but if I don't do this, I start to get into unreality, and that's really not a good thing. With God, honesty is always the best policy.

The result

The Lord gave Hannah a lovely baby boy, and she stuck to her vow and gave him to the Lord. He was called Samuel, was raised in the temple and became a prophet in Israel at a time when the people desperately needed spiritual leadership. His life was quite amazing and the Bible says of him that 'the LORD . . . let none of his words fall to the ground' (1 Samuel 3:19 NIV) – his prophecies were spot on his whole life through.

Oh, and after Hannah gave birth to Samuel, she was blessed with three more sons and two daughters!

Conclusion

Hannah let her desperation fuel her prayers. Everything seemed against her, but instead of panicking or giving up, she pressed in to God. The answer didn't come overnight, but she stayed her course, determined to rely on God alone. She would rather wait for a miracle than go for a cheap fix. Within it all, she demonstrates great integrity. She will not wear a mask before God or man, knowing that God isn't shaken by emotions or grief, but actually treasures her cries and keeps her tears in His 'bottle' (Psalm 56:8).

Ask yourself

- How will you respond to desperate situations? Will you cut yourself off from God, or will you let the situation push you further in to Him?

5

Solomon Asks for the Right Stuff

Setting the scene

The wisdom of Solomon! Thousands of years after the man lived, he's still a household name. But I wonder if you've ever read how he got to be so wise.

Solomon was the son of the very famous and successful King David. Whether it was killing giants, worshipping God or uniting the people, David had done all things well. As David was on his deathbed, his children began jostling for position – the prospect of being king of not just a powerful nation, but God's nation, was an appealing one. Amidst the arguments, David decided that Solomon should be king after him, and so it was. Barely a man, Solomon found himself the head of the most powerful kingdom in the region. Exciting? Yes, but also very scary! Solomon understood this.

One night while Solomon was in Gibeon, the LORD God appeared to him in a dream and said, 'Solomon, ask for anything you want, and I will give it to you.'

Solomon answered: 'My father David, your servant, was honest and did what you commanded. You were always loyal to him, and you gave him a son who is now king. LORD God, I'm your servant, and you've made me king in my father's place. But I'm very young and know so little about being a leader. And now I must rule your chosen people, even though there are too many of them to count. Please make me wise and teach me the difference between right and wrong. Then I will know how to rule your people. If you don't, there is no way I could rule this great nation of yours.'

God said: 'Solomon, I'm pleased that you asked for this. You could have asked to live a long time or to be rich. Or you could have asked for your enemies to be destroyed. Instead, you asked for wisdom to make right decisions. So I'll make you wiser than anyone who has ever lived or ever will live. I'll also give you what you didn't ask for. You'll be rich and respected as long as you live, and you'll be greater than any other king. If you obey me and follow my commands, as your father David did, I'll let you live a long time.'

Solomon woke up and realised that God had spoken to him in the dream. He went back to Jerusalem and stood in front of the sacred chest, where he offered sacrifices to please the Lord and sacrifices to ask his blessing. Then Solomon gave a feast for his officials.

(1 Kings 3:5–15)

Insights

Put yourself in Solomon's shoes. He's just become king, but it's been very messy. One of his own brothers raced him to the throne, and everyone's feeling unsettled and unsafe. They're looking for a strong leader to bring them through this anxious time and Solomon is that man. Feel the pressure!

Shortly after his reign begins, the Lord appears to Solomon in his sleep and says this amazing thing about giving him whatever he asks for. What a position to be in! What would you ask for? Bigger muscles? Loads of money? The perfect partner? The possibilities are endless.

In a situation like this, the thing that's asked for says a lot about the person who asks. And Solomon asks for an understanding heart. Why do you think he asked for this?

First and foremost, Solomon knew where he was at: he was barely an adult and there were lots of things he didn't know. A sober understanding of yourself is a very precious thing and not easy to come by. I know what I'm like – if I do one thing badly I disqualify myself, but if I do one thing well I think I've arrived! Not so Solomon. He realised that he was immature and that without God's wisdom he'd make a mess of things.

It's OK to be immature and to admit that to God. He won't get angry. Imagine if He did – it would be crazy. Imagine a parent getting annoyed with their baby because she keeps falling over as she's learning to walk!

Solomon was thrust into his reign early in life, and the first thing he did was to acknowledge his inadequacy before God, and that was the best thing he could have done. If you feel inadequate before God about anything He's called you to do, just tell Him.

Importantly, though, Solomon doesn't leave it there. He knows that God doesn't want him just to get by and do OK; He wants to pour out blessings on him, like He did with David. Solomon isn't embarrassed about this; he doesn't try to cover over God's blessing and explain it away. Instead he boasts about it.

When you feel inadequate before a certain God-given task,

it's ever so important that you move on from there to a place of confidence in God's favour towards you. Say to God, 'I know You love me because You gave Your only Son for me, to die in my place' (see Romans 5:8; John 3:16). Say to God, 'I know You will fulfil Your promises to me because all of Your promises are "Yes" and "Amen" in Christ Jesus' (see 2 Corinthians 1:20). Say to God, 'I know You will bless me because You've already blessed me with every spiritual blessing in the heavenly places and You won't change Your mind' (see Ephesians 1:3; Numbers 23:19).

Once you've been strengthened *in the truth*, then you're in a good position to ask God for what's needed. If you're not convinced of God's favour, then your prayers will be weak and flimsy, and even double-minded (read James 1:5–8 to see what this will lead to). If you *are* convinced of God's favour, then not only are you ready to pray with confidence, but you're ready to wait *unswervingly* for the answers, not being knocked off course even if some surprises come your way.

So Solomon asks God for an understanding heart. What a wonderful moment. What a choice use of an open request. Solomon wants to rule well. He doesn't want to blow it and mess up people's lives, so he asks God for wisdom. Now I realise that Solomon's situation is a little bit special (how many of us have had a visit in the night offering us whatever we ask for?), but throughout the Bible there's a general principle that develops around this subject of asking and receiving.

As we saw in Chapter 2, when the Israelites are about to be destroyed by God in the wilderness, Moses pleads with God on the grounds of His promises, and God shows mercy. The New Testament encourages strong confidence in prayer. Jesus promises that whatever we ask for in His name, we will get, and those who persevere in their requests without losing heart will receive what they desire (see Matthew 7:7–8; John 14:13–14; and many more).

The lesson here is that God loves to give good gifts to His children. Let me say it again – God loves to give good gifts to His children. Just as a normal dad loves hearing his children ask for good things, and then does all he can to get those things for them, so it is with God (the difference being that He can do anything, so there are no limits). This might sound obvious, but I believe it needs to be grasped on a deeper level, to be understood to the extent where it becomes our great delight to ask and ask and ask, knowing that God loves to hear us and grant us our requests. I'm convinced that the longer our lists of answered prayer, the more greatly God is glorified in our lives (see the link between John 15:5, 7 and 8). Sometimes we develop a strange reverse psychology where we think God is glorified if nothing happens, because that shows how faithful we are to keep believing even though nothing's happening. But think about that a bit more carefully. The thing that glorifies God in that scenario is not that the prayer hasn't been answered yet, but that the asker *is still believing God for the answer even though it's taking a while*! This demonstrates clearly that the situation will reach its glorious conclusion when the prayer is finally answered.

Finally, have another quick think about what Solomon asks for. He asks for an understanding heart, or wisdom – knowing the right thing to do in any given situation, seeing people and problems from an accurate perspective. What a gift to possess! The Bible tells us that nothing you desire can be compared to wisdom (see Proverbs 3:15). Because of this you would be wise to put it at the top of your list. You might think you have a better challenger for the top spot, but if you do, the above reference tells you that you're wrong. If you think wisdom isn't up to much, then you haven't seen it for what it is.

It's worth taking some time out to read through the book of Proverbs in the Bible and see the way wisdom is talked about. That should be enough to inspire you to get wisdom up there at least in the top three! Wisdom will have a massive impact on your relationships with people, it will equip you to make shrewd and insightful decisions that you won't regret, and it will radically affect the direction your life takes and your equipping for the tasks God gives you.

Follow Solomon's pattern in this matter, because the Bible teaches that we all have a destiny – and although it might not be ruling a nation, your destiny fits just as perfectly into God's sovereign plan as Solomon's did, so don't despise it by being flippant. 'Wisdom shouts in the street, she lifts her voice in the square . . . Turn to my reproof, behold, I will pour out my spirit on you; I will make my words known to you' (Proverbs 1:20, 23 NASB). Wisdom is so keen to come into your life, and the promise is that as you search for her in the same way you would for treasure, she will certainly be found by you.

The result

God is so pleased with Solomon's request that He grants him not only wisdom, but a whole load of other things as well. The kingdom of Israel reaches unprecedented heights of prosperity and glory under his reign, and God more than equips him for the job. It must be noted that things don't end well, as Solomon rejects the wisdom of God on a certain issue and brings the nation of Israel into a very dangerous place. But this only emphasises the need for continually seeking God for wisdom and obeying what He reveals.

The conclusion

Solomon faces up to the pressure he's under by acknowledging his inexperience and immaturity before God. Then *he takes his stand on God's promised favour*, and doesn't waver in regard to his confidence in God. He requests an understanding heart, recognising that God is able to shed light on all manner of mysteries and perplexing situations in a supernatural way. God delights in his request (as He does in all good requests), and grants Solomon what he asks for and much more.

Ask yourself

- Will you give wisdom a top spot on your prayer list, so that you can prosper and do well in all that God has for you?

6

Elijah Shakes a Nation

Setting the scene

Elijah was a prophet who appeared in Israel during dark times. Under the leadership of King Ahab and his awful wife Jezebel, Israel had become a nation of idol worship, immorality and murder. Of those who had remained faithful to the Lord, many had been killed and the lucky ones were being hidden in caves to escape the onslaught. It was a time of desperation and something (or someone) drastic was needed. The curtains are drawn back, and onto centre stage steps Elijah.

Elijah was a prophet from Tishbe in Gilead. One day he went to King Ahab and said, 'I'm a servant of the living LORD, the God of Israel. And I swear in his name that it won't rain until I say so. There won't even be any dew on the ground.'
(1 Kings 17:1)

For three years no rain fell in Samaria [the capital of Israel], and there was almost nothing to eat anywhere. The LORD said to Elijah, 'Go and meet with King Ahab. I will soon make it rain.' So Elijah went to see Ahab.
(1 Kings 18:1–2)

Elijah told Ahab, 'Get something to eat and drink. I hear a heavy rain coming.'

Ahab left, but Elijah climbed back to the top of Mount Carmel. Then he stooped down with his face almost to the ground and said to his servant, 'Look towards the sea.'

The servant left. And when he came back he said, 'I looked, but I didn't see anything.' Elijah told him to look seven more times.

After the seventh time the servant replied, 'I see a small cloud coming this way. But it's no bigger than a fist.'

Elijah told him, 'Tell Ahab to get his chariot ready and start home now. Otherwise, the rain will stop him.'

A few minutes later, it got very cloudy and windy, and rain started pouring down.
(1 Kings 18:41–45)

Elijah was just as human as we are, and for three and a half years his prayers kept the rain from falling. But when he did pray for rain, it fell from the skies and made the crops grow.
(James 5:17–18)

Insights

I hope you understand the size of what you've just read. Elijah prayed, and a whole country had no rain for three and a half years. Then he prayed again, and the rain came down. An entire nation was shaken by his prayers. Oh my goodness. How on earth did he come to this place of authority in prayer? I'll show you four keys.

The first and most important place to start was that he was 'just like us' (James 5:17 NIV). It's important that you begin here. This shows straight away that little old you can become big old you. Why? Because Elijah did. I'm not saying that your calling and his are the same, but whatever your destiny is, you can grow in it to a place of profound authority. As you pray about the things into which God's directing you, you can move mountains. Surely this isn't out of your reach. Didn't Jesus say that faith the size of a mustard seed would uproot whole mountains (see Matthew 17:20)?

The disciples were often amazed by Jesus' miracles, but He often actually turned the focus onto them and promised that the same authority and power were available to them, as they believed (see Mark 11:20–24; John 14:12; Mark 9:22–23; 4:35–41). Why did He do this? I believe it's because He wanted to get them out of a passive mindset, and encourage them to begin to exercise themselves in pursuit of the same things that He was doing. As I said before, Elijah shook a whole nation with his prayers. Why not you too? Small-mindedness is a curse from which God wants to deliver us. I'm not saying that things don't start small. Of course they do. Jesus is clear about that in Matthew 13:31–32, but notice that in this parable the mustard seed, which is the tiniest seed of all, grows into the tree that's larger than all the other garden plants. We start small, but we grow. We're not called to reach a plateau and level off. No! Paul talks about the 'upward call of God in Christ Jesus' (Philippians 3:14 NASB). God is always calling us upward into a greater and greater experience of heaven and His kingdom. Hallelujah! This is for all those who are like Elijah – weak, frail and human. Wow.

The second key is to do with who Elijah was. We read in 1 Kings 17:1 that Elijah was a servant of the living God. This is the place of spiritual authority. Jesus said about Himself,

'. . .the Son of Man did not come to be served, but to serve. . .' and we read in Philippians 2 that Jesus' commitment to the Father's will was so fundamental that He was 'obedient to the point of death'. This is true servanthood. It's deep and radical, and cuts right into the core of who we are and what makes us tick. As followers of Jesus, we must take our place as those who are here not to be served but to serve a purpose far greater than ourselves.

When God entrusts people with spiritual authority, He looks for trustworthiness. So I'll ask you a question. Can God trust you? Do you serve Him, or do you serve yourself? I'm not asking if you go to church, or even if you play in a worship band or serve in a kids' club. I'm asking you what you're about deep down – God's purposes or your own? This might sound a bit harsh, but maybe a lot of Christians wonder why there's no power, and yet the truth is that they're really just doing their own thing. That will explain it, and save a lot of wondering.

Once you've come to the place where you say, 'Yes, I'm here to serve and not be served,' then you need to be confident and strong regarding who you are, which is the third key. Elijah knew who he was. This might sound obvious, but it's actually important, because you can make the decision to serve, but then get into a kind of false humility, where you never realise who you are and never take hold of the authority that's given to the position of the servant of God. If you're serving His purposes, then you should know that He will back you up! Now that *is* worth getting fired up about. Your expectations should be rising. It would be crazy for a master to send a servant out on a mission, and then for the servant to find that his master doesn't back him up when he comes to do his task. When you pray, it's ever so important that you know who you are. Don't apologise for coming into God's presence; He's the One who's calling you in, so that He can assign you your mission and assist you as you serve Him.

If you're doing God's will, then you need to be able to stand in confidence before Him and make bold requests. If you're only asking Him to do little things, then why bother even praying about it? Do it yourself! This nation needs shaking and no amount of nice stuff that we do will shake it sufficiently. What we need is a move of God, an awesome outpouring of His Holy Spirit, and take it from me, no person can conjure that up. Only a gracious answer to fervent and bold prayers will do the trick. Servant of God, know who you are and stand before God and man with boldness, as Elijah did. Feel free to say, 'I am a servant of the living Lord, the God of Israel.'

The final key is unswerving expectation. It's one thing to be sent off on a mission from God and be confident, but what about when things don't seem to be going to plan? What do you do then? Do you waver? A lot of people do, and I'm sure we've all felt that temptation. Look at Elijah. He prophesies that the rain is about to start falling, and sends King Ahab on his way, so that he doesn't get drenched. After this he goes to pray, and *obviously expects the answer*. This is good. When you pray and don't really expect God to grant you your request, you're wasting your time. Prayer was never meant to be that way. Throughout the Bible there are amazing promises about prayer which make it very clear that our requests are supposed to be granted. Because of this, we're meant to be looking for the answers to our prayers. But what should we do when nothing seems to be coming? Look at what Elijah did. He sent his servant seven times to go and look for the answer to his prayer, and remained steadfast throughout the whole test. What if he had stopped praying after six times? Who knows? But what I do know is that he kept going and the answer came.

I want to urge you not to swerve in your confidence before God. Jesus told some parables on prayer in Luke 11:5–8 and 18:1–8, both of which teach that some prayers get answered for one reason and one reason alone, and that is that the person who's praying just refuses to give up until the request is granted. Before you think that's rude, let me say that Jesus was *commending* the people in these parables, not *correcting* them. In the famous promise 'Ask and you will receive, search and you will find, knock and the door will be opened for you' (Luke 11:9), each time in the Greek the words 'ask', 'search' and 'knock' are written in what's called the present-continuous tense, which means that a more correct translation would be, 'Keep on asking and you will receive, keep on searching and you will find, keep on knocking and the door will be opened.' Aha! Now there's a key for you. Elijah knew it, Jesus knew it and now you know it. Put it into practice and you will be mighty in prayer.

The result

The rain came down! Enough said.

The conclusion

Elijah was just like us, and yet he grew in God, to a place where his prayers shook a whole nation. He used his frailties to throw himself on God in total dependence, which led to immense supernatural power being displayed through him. He turned his back on living for himself, but took his place as servant of the most high God. Not only this, but he knew who he was and took a stand on it, declaring it boldly to the king of Israel. Finally, when it came to a time of serious testing and pressure regarding what seemed to be unanswered prayer, he stayed on his knees and kept looking expectantly for the hand of God to move – which it did.

Ask yourself

- Do you know who you are? If you're a servant of the Lord, sent by Him and on His business, then are you acting like it, speaking like it and praying like it?
- Will you pray and pray and then pray again until the answer comes?

7

Elisha Sees the Unseen

Setting the scene

If you think Elijah's good, just wait till you read about Elisha! This amazing prophet did twice as many miracles. He was the successor to Elijah, the man you've just read about. At the time of this story, there were constant little wars being fought out between Israel and her neighbours; it was very unsettled in that region. (Sound familiar?) In this particular story, the Israelites were having some trouble with the Syrians, which is where we'll pick it up.

Time after time, when the king of Syria was at war against the Israelites, he met with his officers and announced, 'I've decided where we will set up camp.'

Each time, Elisha would send this warning to the king of Israel: 'Don't go near there. That's where the Syrian troops have set up camp.' So the king would warn the Israelite troops in that place to be on guard.

The king of Syria was furious when he found out what was happening. He called in his officers and asked, 'Which one of you has been telling the king of Israel our plans?'

'None of us, Your Majesty,' one of them answered. 'It's an Israelite named Elisha. He's a prophet, so he can tell his king everything – even what you say in your own room.'

'Find out where he is!' the king ordered. 'I'll send soldiers to bring him here.'

They learnt that Elisha was in the town of Dothan and reported it to the king. He ordered his best troops to go there with horses and chariots. They marched out during the night and surrounded the town.

When Elisha's servant got up the next morning, he saw that Syrian troops had the town surrounded. 'Sir, what are we going to do?' he asked.

'Don't be afraid,' Elisha answered. There are more troops on our side than on theirs.' Then he prayed, 'LORD, please help him to see.' And the LORD let the servant see that the hill was covered with fiery horses and flaming chariots all around Elisha.
(2 Kings 6:8–17)

Insights

What a story! Put yourself in the position of Elisha's servant. You get up in the morning, go out for a stroll, and find that you're completely surrounded by your enemy – not a good start to the day. Understandably, he goes straight to his master and says, 'Sir, what are we going to do?'

How does Elisha respond? Well, he tells his servant not to worry, and says that *they* are actually the ones in the majority, with an army that outnumbers the enemy. The servant must have thought, 'OK, that sounds great, but reality suggests otherwise. I've just been out there and *we're* the ones who are surrounded.' Maybe the servant wished that Elisha wouldn't be so *spiritual* all the time!

Why does Elisha's assessment of the situation seem so different from his servant's? Simple. Elisha can see the spirit realm and his servant can't. They're operating on different levels of reality!

Elisha knows what his servant needs more than anything else: he needs a revelation. This is wonderful. The Bible is full of amazing statements about how God has blessed us with every spiritual blessing, and how God can do more than we can even ask or imagine, etc., but the issue is, *do we see this*? It's one thing to have someone say something to us, or to read something, but it's altogether different to *see* it.

Elisha told his servant two things. The first was not to be afraid. The second was that they were in the majority. But that wasn't enough. He then had to *pray* for his servant, that God would open his eyes to these realities – and when that happened, boy oh boy, was he let in on a whole new wavelength!

Can you imagine what happened in the servant's mind when God answered the prayer? As he suddenly saw reality from God's perspective, he would have gone from feeling like a victim to feeling like a conqueror, from being on the edge of defeat to being on the edge of victory, from being drained of all strength to being more pumped than you can imagine. This is the power of revelation. I'll say it again: this is the power of revelation.

The things in the Bible that God says He has already done for us are, in all honesty, quite staggering. We're forgiven, justified, adopted, equipped, commissioned, loved, affirmed, empowered, blessed – the list just goes on. But what we really need is to *see* this. These blessings can all be sitting there like that heavenly army on the side of the hill, but until we see them, lined up and ready for action, glowing with the glory and fire of God, we will never realise the victory and splendour that's at our fingertips.

So what do we do? We pray, of course. That's what this book is about, and I hope that you're beginning to see the importance of this. Elisha prayed and the servant's eyes were opened. We follow suit. The answer may take time, or it may come quickly, but we pray until it comes. The revelation may come in one fell swoop, as in this story, or it may come bit by bit, in dribs and drabs, with ever increasing glory; but however it comes and in whatever way, it comes *as we ask for it*.

People have two sets of eyes. There are our physical eyes and then there are the eyes of our heart/mind (see Ephesians 1:18; 2 Corinthians 4:4). In the Bible, the apostle Paul prays that the eyes of our hearts will be enlightened. He prays this because we're born dull to the things of the Spirit (see Ephesians 2:1–3), and even once we're born again, it's almost like the beginning of a journey, where we come to increasing revelation and understanding of spiritual things (see 2 Corinthians 3:18). We need more and more revelation, so that we can see with the eyes of our hearts what's going on in the realm of the spirit.

This might sound a bit spooky and weird, but don't worry, the things that God shows us by revelation will never disagree with the Bible, so you can feel safe with it. It won't be that God shows you a new way of getting saved! In fact, most of the things God reveals will be the very stuff of the Bible; it's just that it will be brought to life and power as we really get to see it.

Maybe you struggle to believe that God really loves you. What do you need? *Revelation* of God's love. Maybe you're worried that God will give up on you. What do you require?

Revelation of God's faithfulness. Jesus said that as we know the truth, the truth will set us free (John 8:31–32). We get to *know* the truth by thinking about it, ordering our life in the light of it, obeying it, and asking God constantly to open our eyes to see it in all its glory. Wow!

Before you start thinking that all this revelation stuff is just too spiritual for you to get . . . if you're a Christian, then you've already *had* the most important revelation. The other stuff I'm talking about here just backs up the Big Revelation, which is that Jesus is the Son of God and has saved you through His death and resurrection. You might say, 'I didn't get a revelation of that I just believed it.' But I would say back to you that you could never have believed it if you hadn't had a revelation of it. You see, the gospel isn't something that you can understand or believe without revelation, and *revelation isn't a tingly feeling; it's a realisation*. You realise that something is true which you didn't realise before. Simple, eh? Be encouraged. If you're a Christian, you're already a traveller on the revelation road!

Perhaps the most striking example of this in the Bible is John the Baptist, who had the job of getting people ready to meet Jesus. He was Jesus' cousin, and their mums were also close friends. I'm suggesting that they'd probably grown up together. But do you know what? John didn't have a clue that Jesus was the Son of God until the Holy Spirit gave him a revelation! You can read the story in John 1:29–34. If John needed revelation to see who Jesus really was, so do we. So let's go for it and ask for more and more revelation.

I know that for me, it's one of the things that I ask for more than anything else. You see, I hate that saying which talks about 'being too heavenly minded to be of any earthly use'.

I'm sure the person who first said it meant well, and had probably just bumped into someone really superspiritual and superannoying, *but* what I do know is that the person who is earthly minded will be of no eternal use on this planet. He'll be crippled by the sin and the pain in the world, overwhelmed by the need and bogged down by the stress. He'll feel surrounded and beaten because all he can see is what is temporary. I can't live like this. I just can't. I need to see the glory of God in a way that's so much more than imagination or positive thinking; I need, by the power of the Holy Spirit, to be let in on the stuff of heaven. If I'm starved of that, I'll go under – it's as simple as that. Open our eyes, Lord!

The result

The army advances, and as they do so Elisha prays that God will strike them blind (a reverse miracle), and this happens. Elisha then informs the army that they've taken a wrong turn and leads them to Israel's capital city, where he prays that their eyes will be opened again. Their sight is restored and they find themselves in the middle of the enemy's capital city! A brilliant victory for God's people.

The conclusion

Elisha isn't fazed by a violent assault, for one reason: his eyes are open to the spiritual realm. He's able to see the greatness of God and the greatness of God's support, even when the enemy is closing in. He prays for his servant to have the same revelation, which God graciously gives. The truth that to be with God is to be in the majority strikes home with amazing force, just by one bit of revelation. I doubt the servant ever looked at life in the same way after this.

Ask yourself

- How will you make sure that you pray for God's under-standing about situations for yourself or someone else, even when you feel under attack?
- Will you make it a regular thing to pray for revelation in order for Bible truths to hit you with fresh impact?

8

Mary Lets God Win

Setting the scene

Imagine that you're a teenage girl (if you are one, then don't worry about imagining it!) and you're at home doing some housework (which, if you're a teenager of any gender, may take all your powers of imagination). Suddenly an angel turns up in your house and tells you some amazing news about you becoming pregnant and giving birth to the Son of God, even though you've never had sex. This is what happened to Mary the mother of Jesus. As you can imagine, it was quite a shock, not to mention the fact that she was engaged to a local carpenter who would have been a bit confused and suspicious, to say the least. How would you respond? Let's take up the story from Luke 1:26.

> . . .God sent the angel Gabriel to the town of Nazareth in Galilee with a message for a virgin named Mary. She was engaged to Joseph from the family of King David. The angel greeted Mary and said, 'You are truly blessed! The Lord is with you.'

Mary was confused by the angel's words and wondered what they meant. Then the angel told Mary, 'Don't be afraid! God is pleased with you, and you will have a son. His name will be Jesus. He will be great and will be called the Son of God Most High. The Lord God will make him king, as his ancestor David was. He will rule the people of Israel for ever, and his kingdom will never end.'

Mary asked the angel, 'How can this happen? I am not married!'

The angel answered, 'The Holy Spirit will come down to you, and God's power will come over you. So your child will be called the holy Son of God. Your relative Elizabeth is also going to have a son, even though she is old. No one thought she could ever have a baby, but in three months she will have a son. Nothing is impossible for God!'

Mary said, 'I am the Lord's servant! Let it happen as you have said.' And the angel left her.
(Luke 1:26–38)

Insights

Where shall I start? Because a lot of us are familiar with this story, it's easy to lose the disgrace of it among Christmas carols and fairy lights – but we mustn't do that. This story is about as full of social shame and stigma as anything you could read about in *Hello* or *OK*!

Of course, in twenty-first-century England it's no big deal if someone gets pregnant before they're married, but in first-century Palestine it was a massive deal. Not only this, but her fiancé, Joseph, who would have known that he wasn't the father of this baby, would obviously have had some questions to ask! In fact, we're told later on that he fully intended to break off the engagement until he was visited by an angel who confirmed that this really was a miraculous pregnancy. What I'm getting at here is that this angelic visit to Mary triggered some serious aggro for her. Everyone, and I mean everyone, would have been up in arms about this baby, and she would have had to face some very angry people. Mary would have realised this, I'm sure, but look at her response to the angel's news: 'I am the Lord's servant! Let it happen as you have said.' Mary was utterly surrendered to the will of God.

'Submit' and 'surrender' are words that are usually associated with war, or wrestling, or some kind of fight. The reason why I want to focus here on surrender in prayer is that there are times when God's will causes a genuine conflict within, as we think about the consequences of obeying Him.

I'm sure all kinds of thoughts went through Mary's mind as the angel told her God's plan. It's amazing how many thoughts can travel through the human mind in a matter of seconds, isn't it? 'What about Joseph? This will really hurt him. This will be the end of our relationship. He'll never believe me. What about my parents? How will they cope with the disgrace? This will devastate them. They'll never believe me. What about the village? Everyone will be talking and laughing. They'll never believe me. . .' The list goes on.

Anxiety, fear and pride are three of the main factors that cause this internal battle, and those three factors are like three stalks coming out of one root – that one root being *unbelief*, the real enemy.

Unbelief will throw up every kind of objection when it comes to obeying God. It's vital that you understand this. Unbelief appears so *rational*, which is one of the biggest problems with it, when all it is, really, is *rebellious*.

So what do you do? Well, in order to come to a place of *joyful submission* to the will of God, unbelief must be fought, and the only thing that can overcome it is genuine faith. Now faith isn't hype, or positive thinking, or anything else as low as that. It's 'being sure of what we hope for and certain of what we do not see' (Hebrews 11:1 NIV), and it's utterly rooted in the Word of God, especially His glorious promises.

I will now show you one particular promise which is especially effective against unbelief; in fact in military terms it's like a nuclear warhead, so get ready. The promise is that God's will is good, pleasing and perfect (Romans 12:2). Now follow me here. Remember the three stalks of unbelief? Well, all of them get destroyed as we use this promise.

Pride gets destroyed because God's will is good. In the original Greek language, this word for 'good' means 'that which is beneficial in its effect' – it benefits us. So you can tell your pride that if it suggests for a minute that it knows a better, more beneficial way than God's saying, then it's lying. Drop dead, pride!

Fear gets destroyed because God's will is pleasing. What is fear rooted in? It's rooted in the lie that if we lose respect, loved ones or nice things, we'll become a saddo. But hold on a minute! God's will is pleasing; it will result in fullness of joy, deeper than any fleeting pleasure. Fear, you can't scare me!

Anxiety gets destroyed because God's will is perfect. This Greek word for 'perfect' denotes 'completeness, lacking nothing'. What does anxiety try to rule over us with? Threats that we'll miss out on some kind of future fulfilment. Forget it! God's will is abundant and complete, and as we submit to that, all good things come in their perfect time. The amazing truth is that we can be a worry-free zone!

I hope you're seeing this now. Used properly, this stuff is pure-prayer-dynamite. I'm not saying that we'll never be bombarded by fear or anxiety when we're in God's will; on the contrary, we most certainly will (see Ephesians 6:12). The issue is that we don't take orders from those things, but instead surrender to God's will.

Mary seems to have realised that God doesn't suggest things on the spur of the moment, or in some kind of rash way, but that He causes every tiny event of history to work towards His ultimate purpose (see Ephesians 1:11). Everything is perfectly thought out by Him, and even the things which cause temporary pain result in an eternal glory that can't be measured (see 2 Corinthians 4:17). Mary understood the wisdom of God, and that although obeying Him would be painful, it would be a lot less painful than disobeying Him. She weighed up the situation, sided with God, and prayed, 'Let it happen as you have said.' Good decision!

But look what happened. As she submitted fearlessly to God's will and prayed that prayer of submission, she was overshadowed by the Holy Spirit and then the miracle took place. As you honestly pray out this kind of prayer, you will be overshadowed by the Holy Spirit; He will overshadow your complexities, insecurities, barriers, everything that keeps you away from God. That's not to say that all your problems and issues will disappear, but they'll no longer be overshadowing you, and that's massive.

We all want victory. We all want triumph. These things come on a certain path. As we submit and surrender (the language of defeat), we can then go on to victory and triumph. We must be overcome by God before we overcome with God. Mary did, and she became a hero of faith.

Prayers of surrender are very precious to God. They're worth praying often, because other things can very quickly get a place in our hearts and begin to mean too much to us. Prayers of surrender help us to keep things in perspective, and to remember that it's the Lord whom we serve.

The will of God can sometimes seem like a heavy thing, but check out these other explosive promises. In 1 John 5:3 (NIV), the apostle tells us that the commands of God 'are not burdensome'. In Matthew 11:28–30 (NIV) Jesus says, 'Come to me, all you who are weary and burdened, and I will give you rest . . . For my yoke is easy and my burden is light.' The devil will often come to us, just like he came to Eve in the garden of Eden (Genesis 3:1–6), and make God out to be a spoilsport. He'll dress up God's commands in heavy clothing and make *his* ways appear shiny and bright. But you know what? He's been doing that since Eden. Not only is he a liar, but he's the father of lies (see John 8:44). Don't believe him! As soon as you submit to God, His wonderful will becomes obviously delightful.

The result

Mary got to carry God around in her womb for nine months! She was trusted with the baby Jesus, to nurture and care for Him in His formative years. On top of all that, her fiancé married her, and didn't leave her.

The conclusion

Mary trusted God entirely. There was no holding back. Her respect, dignity, future – everything was at risk because of

God's plan. Her prayer was simple but heartfelt. It was pure submission. As a result, she has become a blessed hero of the faith.

Ask yourself

• How will you demonstrate your belief that God's will is the best?

9

The Other Mary Keeps Quiet

Setting the scene

It looked like the perfect situation: food, friendship and laughter. But appearances can be deceiving. Jesus was visiting three of His friends – Lazarus and his sisters Martha and Mary. Around dinnertime, everything *seems* to be going well, until the hidden stress levels reach fever pitch and explode. Let's pick up the story.

Mary . . . sat down in front of the Lord and was listening to what he said. Martha was worried about all that had to be done. Finally, she went to Jesus and said, 'Lord, doesn't it bother you that my sister has left me to do all the work by myself? Tell her to come and help me!'

The Lord answered, 'Martha, Martha! You are worried and upset about so many things, but only one thing is necessary. Mary has chosen what is best, and it will not be taken away from her.'
(Luke 10:39–42)

Insights

Question: does sitting down in front of the Lord, listening to what He said, qualify as a prayer? I'm not sure, but being with Jesus and keeping your mouth shut is something so precious that it definitely deserves a chapter! Obviously we don't have the physical Jesus, as Mary did, but we do have His very real presence through the Holy Spirit.

So what's the point in silence? I'll give you a quote by Kathryn Kuhlman, a famous healing evangelist from the last century, that might show you the point: 'He comes in when you're quiet.' Wow. In her meetings, where amazing miracles took place, she would sometimes insist that everyone was silent (and we're talking hundreds and, on occasion, thousands of people) while they waited for the Holy Spirit. Sometimes it would take a long time, but after a while all heaven broke loose as God came down. That's the point.

Being silent before God is very profound. When you consider that the human tongue is the only thing that humanity can't tame and that it has the power to set our life on course for hell (see James 3:1–12), and that we'll be held to account and judged for every careless word we utter (see Matthew 12:36), it surely follows that God loves spending time with us while our mute button is well and truly switched on!

If we're truly to give everything to Jesus, this must include our tongue. This will mean being quiet sometimes. It makes sense, really. One of the ways we relate to Jesus is as a student with a teacher. Now then, which one should do the most talking in that relationship? You've got it! I hope you're seeing the importance of this.

Here are some words from the Bible: 'It's best just to listen when you go to worship. Don't talk before you think or make promises to God without thinking them through. God is in heaven, and you are on earth, so don't talk too much' (Ecclesiastes 5:1–2).

In the book *Celebration of Discipline* Richard Foster says,

> One reason we can hardly bear to remain silent is that it makes us feel so helpless. If we are silent who will take control? God will take control; but we will never let Him take control until we trust Him. Silence is intimately related to trust.[1]

If we can be quiet before God, then we know that we have the freedom just to 'be' before Him; that by Christ's work for us we are free just to be with God. What a wonder.

Let's look at the language Jesus used to describe Mary's silence. There were three little phrases He used. The first is *'what is best'*, the second is *'one thing necessary'* and the third is *'it won't be taken away from her'*.

Just take stock of those for a moment. Mary's actions provoked a high level of praise from Jesus. But you might protest, 'Why such praise? How can Jesus say she chose what was *best*? She didn't even do anything!' That's probably just the point. Perhaps one of our biggest problems is that we often think that we have to do 'oh so much' for God, when He's really quite able Himself! Our hyperactivity and constant chitter-chatter could be one of the biggest barriers to seeing God move. Isaiah 64:1–4 is a passage which talks about God moving in awesome power. The passage mentions how holy and different God is, and it illustrates this by describing Him as the One 'who acts on behalf of those who wait for him'

---

[1] Richard Foster, *Celebration of Discipline*, Hodder and Stoughton 1980, page 88.

(NIV). Please understand that phrase. It talks about the activity of God, and if there's one thing the church is ever in need of from Jesus' time right up to the present day, it's exactly that: God's activity. Not good ideas or scurrying around, but a move of God. And on whose behalf does God act? Those who babble a lot? No. Those who run around here and there? No. He acts on behalf of those who wait for Him. The point is not that we stop our activity, or even that we become like silent statues. The point is this: that deep in our being we understand that God is sufficient, and we don't subconsciously try to make up something that we feel is lacking in Him or in us by babbling and running around.

Mary had got that, but Martha didn't seem to. As A. W. Tozer said,

> Religion has accepted the monstrous heresy that noise, size, activity and bluster make a man dear to God. But we may take heart. To a people caught in the tempest of the last great conflict God says, 'Be still, and know that I am God' (Psalm 46:10), and still He says it, as if He means to tell us that our strength and safety lie not in noise but in silence.[2]

If we're confident in God and His promises, we'll take time to be still before Him, so that we might learn from Him and receive instruction and direction, so that we might then embark on *fruitful* labour and *meaningful* tasks.

There's no doubt that Martha had a good heart; she just wanted to serve Jesus. The thing is, she got the order wrong. If Jesus is talking, then listen. There'll be time for cooking afterwards.

---

[2] A. W. Tozer, *The Pursuit of Glory*, Authentic Lifestyle 1987.

Forgive me for being negative, but Christianity is often very busy but lacking in raw power and heavenly anointing. The most damaging element of this is that we can sometimes be made to feel bad if we're not involved in everything. The thing is, in the Bible things were really quite simple. They seemed content to love God and Jesus, and then love people and tell them about Him. As issues arose in the light of doing that, they would deal with them. The busier the apostles got, the more they focused on Bible study, preaching and prayer (see Acts 6:4). Those things were their priorities and they refused to get distracted from them. They had obviously heard Jesus tell Mary that she had chosen the one thing *necessary*.

Finally, there's this third phrase in which Jesus points out that what she'd gone for would not be '*taken away from her*'. As Mary was quiet before Jesus, she was welcoming Him and cultivating a heart where His word could dwell. Nothing and no one could take that from her. We live in a world full of things that don't last. Holidays and hobbies – though enjoyable – are fleeting. Even the people nearest and dearest to us will one day be taken; that's reality. The presence of Christ, the tangible, glorious presence of Christ, is something that will by no means be taken away from us. Who can separate us from the love of Christ (Romans 8:35–39)?

As you take time to be still before God, don't be surprised if it feels a bit odd at first. You're probably not used to it. Your tongue may well start to panic! But if you're able to develop times of silence before God, you'll be doing a wise thing. You'll be taming the hardest thing to tame. You'll be adopting the proper position of student and not teacher. You'll be aligning yourself to see God act on your behalf. You'll be choosing what is best. And unlike many other things in life, it will not be taken away from you.

The result

Mary was commended, but it seems that both sisters learnt the lesson because they continued following Jesus. They are both now in heaven, where what they once knew only in part they are now enjoying to the full. There's no more tension and misunderstanding between them; all that has gone. Just think, right at this moment they're face to face with the risen Lord Jesus, and they're enjoying the kind of intimacy with Him that's impossible to imagine!

Conclusion

Mary was willing to sit and listen to Jesus, even when her sister was trying to pressurise her to do stuff. Mary didn't move. She knew her priorities, and was even willing to risk accusation and misunderstanding in order to stay at His feet. Jesus praised her for this. Do likewise, and you'll be choosing the best and only necessary thing.

Ask yourself

- How will you cease from striving and develop confidence in Jesus?
- Are you willing to risk misunderstanding and accusation in order to meet Jesus?

10

Jesus on Faith

Setting the scene

A day before this story, Jesus had cursed a tree. I know this sounds a bit strange, but there you go. The morning after He'd done this, He was walking past the tree with His disciples and they pointed out, in shocked voices, that it had actually withered from the roots up! Jesus notices their surprise and takes it as an opportunity to teach them about faith and prayer.

> *Jesus answered saying to them, 'Have you the faith of God? I tell you honestly, whoever says to this mountain, "Be taken up and cast into the sea," and doesn't doubt in his heart, but believes that what he says is going to happen, it shall be granted him. Therefore, I say to you, all things for which you pray and ask, believe that you have received them, and they shall be given to you.'*
> *(Mark 11:22–24)*

Insights

Now, before I start, some of you will say, 'Hold on a minute! This book is about people "just like us". It's not fair to do a chapter on Jesus!' My reply? 'I'm going to do *two* chapters on Him!' I have two reasons. First, although He's obviously unique, He's also the ultimate example of a human living in complete dependence on the Holy Spirit. Philippians 2:7 teaches that although Jesus existed from eternity in the very form of God, when He became a man He 'gave up everything and became a slave, when he became like one of us'. So as a man, He was just like us; if He wasn't, then He couldn't really be a realistic example for us. Second, the teaching that Jesus is giving in the next two chapters is addressed to the disciples, who, as you know, were just like us. I rest my case!

Jesus notices His disciples' surprise at the power of His curse and seizes the moment to challenge unbelief. The disciples had obviously not expected too much to happen to the cursed tree. When Jesus originally cursed it they probably just thought, 'Yeah, tree! That'll teach you. And He'll tell you off again if you don't bear fruit for Him next time!' They hadn't seen the link between things spoken under the anointing of God's Spirit and massive changes on the earth. Jesus wanted to address this.

Something you need to understand is that when you're born again, you get a new spiritual DNA; unbelief is replaced by faith. The faith principle replaces the unbelief principle. More than anything, you're now convinced of God's existence, the truth of the Bible, the gospel message, etc. That underlies everything else. It becomes the deepest thing in you. Praying now makes sense and means something, whereas before, if you did it at all, it used to be talking into the air. This is the foundation of your whole life from now on. It's something God has done and it can't be taken away. Because of this, you always have this deposit of faith with which to pray and by which to live. But when it comes to particular obstacles and issues, as Jesus is describing here, special gifts of faith are often needed to overcome them; and it's this faith I'm referring to in this chapter: *specific faith for specific things.*

Now maybe, when you read the first sentence in the Bible passage above ('Have you the faith of God?'), you thought, 'I don't think my Bible says it like that,' and it probably doesn't. I've put the word-for-word Greek translation in, because in this case it's very important. Your Bible probably reads, 'Have faith in God.' The problem with this is that it puts the emphasis on you to produce faith. The correct translation makes it clear that you need faith from God; it's *His* faith, which He brings as a gift as we get to know Him better. This is why the Bible calls Jesus 'the author and perfecter of our faith' (Hebrews 12:2 NIV).

Over the years there has been a lot of misunderstanding about faith. Some people have taught about it as if it's a matter of the will – if you try hard enough to believe, you'll get the victory. This just doesn't work. Imagine I had some green trousers on and I said to you, 'What colour trousers am I wearing?' Providing you weren't colour blind you would reply, 'Green.' If I then said to you, 'I would really appreciate it if you thought they were red. Can you please now exercise all your faculties to believe that they are, in fact, red?' Now, try as you might to do this for me, you would fail. Why? Because in order truly to believe something, you have to be genuinely convinced. *It's not about trying.* It's not a decision that you make. It's impossible to choose to believe something; you either believe something to be true, or you don't.

Hebrews 11:1 says that faith is 'being sure of what we hope for and certain of what we do not see'. 'Sure' and 'certain' are strong words. Sometimes people get all worked up about things they want from God and say that they're in faith, but they obviously aren't. They may well be in the battle which often precedes faith, but once they're in faith, there's a certainty; they become sure; it's as good as done. Only Jesus can provide this. It's also worth noting that genuine faith is concerned with God, not with itself! Genuine faith is certain about God's will, not worried about how much faith it has. I say this because sometimes people get so worked up about faith that they lose sight of Jesus – the only One who can give us true faith.

The beauty of this is that it shows us faith is something entirely supernatural, and it's as we come to God with an open heart and seek Him for this that it is given to us. As the great healing evangelist Charles Price said,

> If you have salvation, it will be because *He* has imparted it. If you have healing, it will be because of *His* virtue. If you have faith, it will be because faith has flowed out of *His* heart into yours; and that is the only faith that can move your mountain. You can have it; for *He* will give it! Then will you know for sure that the faith – your faith that has made you whole – is a gift from God.[1]

Amen to that!

But look at the results of this faith! This is beautiful, because there are so many 'mountains' before us: the sick so

---

[1] Charles Price, *The Real Faith*, Logos International 1972, page 60.

often don't get healed, salvation is sporadic, growth is slow, and so on. Because of this, we need to sit up at this point and recognise that we're about to be let in on a vital key. As we speak in true faith, we move mountains. The mountains have to move when we're operating in genuine, God-given faith, because the natural cannot resist the supernatural. Earth cannot resist heaven. Which is why, when God said, 'Let there be light' (Genesis 1:3), there had to be light. I know this sounds a bit big and mysterious, but if you just read this teaching straight from the Bible, there can be no other explanation.

In the light of this, let's look at how this links with prayer. Jesus said, 'Therefore I say to you, all things for which you pray and ask, believe that you have received them, and they will be granted you' (Mark 11:24 NASB). Notice that Jesus wants His disciples to do the same stuff as Him, and He's not saying, 'Only I can do this because I am the Son of God.' Then He makes a point of saying that it refers to all things that we pray for. And then He says this remarkable stuff about believing that you've received those things before they've actually been given!

How do we respond to teaching this radical? Well, let me help you by telling you a story. When I first became a youth leader, the spiritual temperature of those I was leading was pretty low. In fact, to be honest, it was heart-breakingly low. I remember coming home one night after being with them, and my heart was heavy. I was burdened with God's heart for them, and I went into my room and began praying. I hope you understand me here: I wasn't just saying my prayers; I was praying. My heart was stretching out to God. I was allowing that burden I felt in my heart for those young people to fuel my prayers to God.

Now, all I can say is that there came a point when, during that prayer time, my pain and burden turned to victorious thanksgiving. It wasn't contrived or forced; I *knew* that there would be a youth group who loved Jesus; I *knew* the kingdom of God was about to break in on those young people. I believed (remember that means I was honestly convinced, not trying to convince myself psychologically) that I had received this, months and years before I saw the evidence with my natural eyes. And so it was. Over the next six years I watched the answer to that prayer unfold before my eyes.

Let me tell you one more story. Someone close to me was feeling paralysed by fear over a situation into which they were pretty convinced God was calling them. This had gone on for a couple of years, and this mountain just would not be moved by reason, or logic, or willpower. It was a bit like Goliath, a mocking giant that was undermining the glory and purposes of God; and as you probably know, that kind of giant only gets killed by genuine, heaven-sent faith missiles that fly through the air and sink into its forehead. We had prayed, but the victory seemed out of our reach.

One day, while I was praying at work (I work at a church, so that kind of thing is allowed!) I brought this situation before God, and as I was praying, I felt a holy anger rise up in me. This situation seemed to be set so utterly against the promises of God. I remember praying and I started saying things like 'Absolutely not! This is *not* right! It's written that we have *not* been given a spirit to make us a slave to fear' (Romans 8:15). And I was swiping with the sword and God was empowering me, and I tell you, a shout from deep in my spirit was coming out and heaven and earth were shaking.

And then, suddenly, that whole shout and anger thing just

went, and it was replaced by a quiet and still confidence. It was done. I was amazed. Now, because I was new to this kind of stuff, I thought that maybe I was making it up, or I'd got it wrong. I also knew that even if I had just got the victory (which is what I was pretty sure had just happened), there was sometimes a time delay between victories in heaven and the actual thing happening on earth, so I decided not to say anything to the person, because I didn't want to make them feel under pressure. I thought I would just watch and see. Anyway, about three weeks later the person came up to me and said that the whole thing had just changed; all they felt was a nervous excitement about serving God in this way, and the paralysing fear had disappeared. Ha ha! Yes! Surely this is what Jesus was talking about, and surely He wants to make this our experience more and more.

The final thing is this: if this faith comes from God, and if God loves to give good gifts to His children (see Matthew 7:11), and if Jesus meant what He taught here, then the obvious response is to ask God for faith and get into the Word of God, which is a breeding ground for faith. Watch what happens!

The result

This whole conversation was sparked by the withered fig tree, demonstrating the reality of Jesus' faith words. Before too long, the disciples had grown in faith to the point where their words were affecting a lot more than fig trees! Read Acts 3 and 4 for details and inspiration.

Conclusion

Jesus isn't satisfied for us to look on in amazement at what He does; He wants to teach us to do the same stuff. He wants us to know that it's all there for us. Can you imagine a church around the world that has learnt how to walk in this kind of faith and uses it to remove godless mountains? The church in the West doesn't have to resign itself to being a spectator as God performs wonderfully in China, South America and middle Africa. Come on! It's all there for us too!

Ask yourself

- Will you refuse just to pray without actually looking for the answers?
- Will you dare to ask for all that you need to see every obstacle moved?

11

Jesus on Forgiveness

Setting the scene

Picture it: Jesus is sitting on a mountain teaching His disciples about all kinds of things – money, anxiety, lust, revenge. The list goes on. Inevitably, He gets onto the subject of prayer. First, He warns them not to be like the hypocrites when they pray, standing on street corners saying deliberately long and fancy prayers to impress other people. He also warns against senseless babbling and chanting. Then He gives them a model of how to order their prayers. This is where we'll pick it up.

Pray, then, in this way:

'Our Father in heaven, help us to honour Your name. Come and set up Your kingdom, come and have Your way on earth – just like You do in heaven. Give us our food for today. Forgive us for doing wrong, as we forgive others. Keep us from being tempted and protect us from the evil one.'

If you forgive others for the wrongs they do to you, your Father in heaven will forgive you. But if you don't forgive others, your Father will not forgive your sins.[1]

---

[1] Matthew 6:9–15, author's own translation.

Insights

Jesus teaches that when we come to God in prayer and we're reminded of certain sins we've committed, we're to do the obvious thing and ask for forgiveness. But it doesn't stop there. Jesus makes a link between being forgiven and forgiving others, and the link He makes is a very strong one. Jesus instructs His disciples that when they come and ask for forgiveness, they will get it in *direct proportion* to the forgiveness they extend to those who have sinned against them. This is very simple, but very searching. Jesus won't let us come and ask for forgiveness and then walk away happy that we're forgiven, without highlighting our own attitudes towards those who have wronged us.

When you read something like that, it's quite easy to skate over it and not take it too seriously. Jesus seems to realise this, and so when He gets to the end of the 'Lord's Prayer', He mentions it again, but this time makes it even clearer. He says, 'If you forgive others for the wrongs they do to you, your Father in heaven will forgive you. But if you don't forgive others, your Father will not forgive your sins.' Pretty clear, isn't it? So why is it such a big deal? In order to answer this, we need to look at (1) what forgiveness is, (2) why it matters to God so much, and (3) how it links with prayer.

So what is forgiveness? Well, to forgive someone is to release them. It's to release them from what they did and not hold on to feelings of bitterness and thoughts of revenge. Forgiveness isn't a feeling; it's a choice. Some people think that it's only when they feel buckets of love for the person who hurt them that they've truly forgiven them. Not so. Forgiveness happens when you say, 'That's it. I choose to release that person. What they did was wrong, but I'm going to leave them with God and not get screwed up and bent on revenge. I'm going to trust that God – in His wisdom – will do what's right.' If it's possible, and appropriate, you then let that person know. That's forgiveness.

The reason why it matters so much to God is probably obvious to you. It's sin that creates the need for forgiveness. God hates sin and God hates everything that comes out of sin, and God is extremely passionate about destroying not only sin, but also the results of sin in our lives.

When God saves us, it's not just to patch us up a bit and send us on our way. His goal is to transform us into the image of Christ (see Ephesians 4:24; 2 Corinthians 3:18), the only person who ever lived free from the power of sin (see Hebrews 4:15). He doesn't want us to live life with a heavy heart, or bitterness, or regrets; these things will only lead to trouble.

I'm sure that, for all of us, there have been people who have hurt us. For some, it might be really big stuff that seems almost unforgivable; for others it might be things that are less obvious but still painful.

It's also important to know that whether we've meant to or not, we're all the cause (to greater and lesser degrees) of other people's pain. It could have been a terrible thing we've done, or it could just be a nasty look; neither one is good. So there's a sober picture: we've all been hurt, and we've all caused pain. Now, if we get all funny about forgiving those who've hurt us and refuse to do it, surely the result is greater pain, sorrow, regret, bitterness, anger and sin – *no matter how justified we might feel*. The horrific thing is that, by our unforgiveness, we could find ourselves opposing God!

Hopefully you see the importance of forgiveness now.

So where does this all fit into prayer? Well, prayer is communicating with God, and Jesus makes it clear that holding back forgiveness greatly affects our harmony with God. How on earth can we honestly ask God to forgive us our sins and then refuse to do that for others? It makes a mockery of the cross and of God's mercy. Jesus is clear that if you withhold forgiveness from anyone, God will withhold forgiveness from you. It's not that you won't be saved if you already are, but there will be a bad effect on your relationship with Him. And you know what? There's no way round this. There are no special cases. This is the way it works, and if you want intimacy with Jesus, then right now I urge you to forgive all those who have ever hurt you – parents, step-parents, friends, strangers – whoever! As you release them, you will be released.

Another prayer connection has to do with our authority. Authority is 'the right to rule', and God wants us to grow in authority in prayer and come to a place of great power in prayer. Now it's very unlikely that God is going to overlook deliberate unforgiveness on your part and allow you to grow worse in this area. It would be very dangerous for Him to do so. Deliberate unforgiveness gives the devil a foothold in your life (see Ephesians 4:26–27), and if you give the devil an inch he'll take a mile. (I use the term 'deliberate unforgiveness' because sometimes we hold on to unforgiveness without realising, and it's only as the Holy Spirit reveals this to us that we have a responsibility to respond.)

The final problem is double-mindedness, which is when you don't make a clear decision on what you're going for, but entertain two ideas that oppose one another. For example, you might love the idea of forgiveness when it comes to your own sins, but hate the idea when it comes to those who have sinned against you. That's a common one! Let's look at what the Bible says about double-mindedness. In James 1:7–8 we're told that the double-minded person should not expect to receive anything in prayer, and later on (chapter 4:8) James tells the double-minded person to cleanse their heart! Strong words. The reason why James is so blunt is that if you let a seed of double-mindedness into your heart, it will eventually turn into a tree of doubt – and believe me, that's not good. James's words are cutting, but if you see him as a surgeon removing a spiritual cancer, it should turn your offence into gratitude.

Let me conclude with a story which shows the power of forgiveness. There was someone who hurt me quite badly a while ago, and although I'd forgiven him in my heart, I'd never let him know – mostly because we weren't really in touch with one another. One night I felt God say that I should write him a letter just to let him know that I completely forgave him for everything. About the same time, that person was woken up in the night and felt the urgent need to forgive his father for all that he'd done to him (which was a lot of bad stuff). Bear in mind that this person was a backslidden Christian at the time he was woken in the night. He prayed a prayer forgiving his father, and then guess what came through the post the next morning. A letter from me, letting him know that I absolutely forgave him for things done *years* ago. Wow! How great and awesome is God! The guilt that person had felt for years about me was lifted off, but only after he had made a decision to forgive the person who had hurt him.

I want you to see that there is such release for us and for those who have wronged us. This is the power and beauty of the gospel. What a wonderful thing Jesus did for us on the cross!

The result

It's not clear how people responded, but it's worth noticing that Jesus ends His sermon by focusing on the fact that you don't get blessed and strengthened by just hearing good sermons. No – it's putting them into practice that counts (see Matthew 7:24–27). You might know God's will and be really excited about it, but move on from there to working it into your life, and you'll find true fruitfulness.

Conclusion

Jesus highlighted the importance of forgiveness when He taught on prayer because it's a decision that we *all* have to make, not a feeling we have to look for. It has massive repercussions for our relationship with God and with others, and it paves the way for an effective prayer life.

Ask yourself

• How will you go about making the right choice to forgive, regardless of how hard it might feel?

12

The Church on Fire and United

Setting the scene

Although the early church was experiencing growth and power, the storm clouds were gathering. Stephen – a godly man – was stoned to death by the Jews because of his powerful Christian life, and that was just the beginning. Let's pick it up here.

> At that time King Herod caused terrible suffering for some members of the church. He ordered soldiers to cut off the head of James, the brother of John. When Herod saw that this pleased the Jewish people, he had Peter arrested . . . and ordered four squads of soldiers to guard him. Herod planned to put him on trial in public after the festival.
>
> While Peter was being kept in jail, the church never stopped praying to God for him.
>
> The night before Peter was to be put on trial, he was asleep and bound by two chains. A soldier was guarding him on each side, and two other soldiers were guarding the entrance to the

jail. Suddenly an angel from the Lord appeared, and light flashed around in the cell. The angel poked Peter in the side and woke him up. Then he said 'Quick! Get up!'

The chains fell off his hands, and the angel said, 'Get dressed and put on your sandals.' Peter did what he was told. Then the angel said, 'Now put on your coat and follow me.' Peter left with the angel, but he thought everything was only a dream. They went past the two groups of soldiers, and when they came to the iron gate to the city, it opened by itself. They went out and were going along the street, when all at once the angel disappeared.

Peter now realised what had happened, and he said, 'I am certain that the Lord sent his angel to rescue me from Herod and from everything the Jewish leaders planned to do to me.' Then Peter went to the house of Mary the mother of John whose other name was Mark. Many of the Lord's followers had come together there and were praying.

Peter knocked on the gate, and a servant named Rhoda came to answer. When she heard Peter's voice, she was too excited to open the gate. She ran back into the house and said that Peter was standing there.

'You are mad!' everyone told her. But she kept saying that it was Peter. Then they said, 'It must be his angel.' But Peter kept on knocking, until finally they opened the gate. They saw him and were completely amazed.

(Acts 12:1–16)

Insights

One of the funniest things about this story has got to be Peter's welcome at the house. He's just been set free by the angel, and when he makes it back to his friends (who are praying for his release), they don't even believe it's him! They think it's more likely to be an angel than to be Peter! It's hilarious, really, and very encouraging. These people really were just like us.

Let's look at this a bit more. Thinking back to the chapter on faith, it's obvious that the church members weren't convinced that Peter would be released, at least not in the near future: it seemed that he was about to follow in James's footsteps and be executed within days. Release down the line was definitely not an option, so it was probably best left as it was. If they'd really believed it, they would have had the door open, waiting for him! So we know that they weren't convinced what God's will was in regard to Peter. Bear in mind that James had just been beheaded, so Peter's execution was well within the realms of possibility. It's therefore instructive to see how they respond. They don't just sit around, but they use what faith they have to stir themselves into prayer. They *know* that God is good. They *know* that nothing is impossible for God. They *know* that God loves Peter. So they just gather together and pray, and God does an extraordinary miracle.

There are two elements to this kind of prayer that I want to highlight, and the first is that they were united. Although it's vital that we get time alone with God, it's also very important that we spend time praying together. Jesus says, 'Whenever two or three of you come together in my name, I am there with you' (Matthew 18:20), and 'When any two of you on earth agree about something you are praying for, my Father in heaven will do it for you' (Matthew 18:19). Jesus points out that there will be a different dynamic – you could say a multiplied dynamic – when we deliberately come together to meet with Him. One reason for this is that God is a united community. Though He is one, He is three, and as we gather together with our hearts united for His glory, it reflects something of Himself and is therefore potent.

Another reason is that one of God's intentions in sending Jesus was not just to save us as individuals and make us individual Holy Spirit temples, but to build us together into a dwelling place for His Spirit (see Ephesians 2:19–22; 1 Peter 2:4–5). Because of this, as we gather together it's like lots of little stones joining in prayer and praise, and as our hearts are united in love for Him and for one another we become one temple and rise up to His throne as a beautiful aroma and reminder of the wonderful work of Jesus. This again touches His heart.

In regard to spiritual warfare, it's also effective because we, as Christ's soldiers, are not acting as lone rangers, little snipers tucked away in corners, but we gather together for full-frontal assaults on the strongholds of the enemy; we charge together and break through barriers and obstacles!

Also, and on a very practical level, we're all different. Because of this, as we gather to pray, one of us will be stirred to pray in a way that another wouldn't, and so something that may have got missed doesn't slip through the net. Another person might receive prophetic insight to guide the praying, which helps all the others, and then another person may get tired, so the others can lift him up and strengthen him, and so on. It's a beautiful picture.

Finally, as Christ's body, we belong not only to God, but also to one another. Because of this, when we're really together in a heartfelt way, *everything* works as it ought, and that includes prayer.

Because of these reasons, let me urge you to meet up with other believers and pray. It may not come easily straight away, but it's worth persevering. None of us are the complete article by ourselves, and it's vital that we realise that. Take the bold step of attending church prayer meetings and inviting a few friends to meet regularly and pray.

This brings me on to the second point. The early church didn't just gather together and say a few casual prayers for Peter. No – they were making fervent and zealous prayer to God for him. What is fervour? Well, the Greek word that's used means 'to stretch out', and it conjures up the image of someone stretching out their whole being towards God in intense desire. Wow.

James 5:16 says that 'the fervent prayer of a righteous man accomplishes much'. I like that. Here are some reasons why it's so effective.

The first is because God is zealous. He is perfect and He is zealous. This shows that to be zealous is to be godly, and we're to ask God that His zeal and His burning desires are rubbed off onto us more and more, and that we are let into something of His passion for His glory. You see this wonderfully in Jesus' life. When He cleared the temple in Jerusalem, the disciples remembered that King David predicted that zeal for God's house would consume the Messiah (see John 2:17; Psalm 69:9). This zeal is for you whether you're a quiet person or a loud person; it's not about personality and has nothing to do with volume and shouting. It's really about caring. It's about caring that God's will be done on the earth; that He gets the glory He deserves and is not despised and kicked against. It's about loving Him in a hot and earnest way. This is zeal, and He loves it.

Sometimes we can get clever and overcomplicated, but there's really no need. Rather a big heart than a big head! It's not that knowledge is useless. On the contrary, it's vital. But if you're going to handle knowledge well, you need a big heart, otherwise you just get all puffed up with pride. Be brave enough to ask yourself some searching questions about your zeal level, and if the answers are disappointing, go to the only One who can make a difference and set about asking Him to change you. Jesus warns that in the end times, 'because of the increase of wickedness, the love of most will grow cold' (Matthew 24:12 NIV). In the world, the more bad things that happen, the more tempting it is just to hide away and get into survival mode; but this is not what God is calling us to. God is calling us to engage with our world, with hearts on fire for His glory, and this starts by engaging with God in fervent prayer, for our neighbours, for our friends and for one another. As we do this, we should expect many miracles to happen. And guess what? Even if we don't expect them to, as we see from this story, they might well happen anyway. So pray! Pray together! Pray with zeal!

The result

As you can probably imagine, the prison was chaos in the morning! No one could figure out where on earth Peter was. Herod was obviously beside himself with rage, and his solution was to put all the guards to death. A short while later, Herod himself came to a gruesome end for taking the glory that God deserved, and Peter went on to be powerfully used by God in seeing the kingdom of Jesus advance and the church prosper. Yes!

Conclusion

Although the church didn't quite know what was going to happen, their knee-jerk response to Peter's imprisonment was to gather together and pray. They prayed with united intensity, and the results were wonderful. Angels appeared, the city gates opened by themselves, Peter became invisible and God's kingdom advanced. Go and do likewise!

Ask yourself

- Will you make it a priority to find other people you can pray with regularly?
- How will you let God's zeal rub off on you so that you become a person who truly cares about God's purposes?

13

Paul and Silas in Painful Praise

Setting the scene

It has been said of the apostle Paul that wherever he went there was either a riot or a revival. This particular story should illustrate that perfectly. Paul is on his second missionary journey, and he's taken Silas along as his partner. They come to a place called Philippi, where people start to get saved. Now in Philippi there's a slave-girl who has a demon which helps her tell the future. Her owners are making a lot of money from her fortune-telling skills, and so when the evil spirit gets driven out of her by Paul and Silas, they get the hump! Let's pick it up there.

When the girl's owners realised that they had lost all chances for making more money, they grabbed Paul and Silas and dragged them into court. They told the officials, 'These Jews are upsetting our city! They are telling us to do things we Romans are not allowed to do.'

The crowd joined in the attack on Paul and Silas. Then the officials tore the clothes off the two men and ordered them to be beaten with a whip. After they had been badly beaten, they were put in jail, and the jailer was told to guard them carefully. The jailer did as he was told. He put them deep inside the jail and chained their feet to heavy blocks of wood.

About midnight Paul and Silas were praying and singing praises to God, while the other prisoners listened. Suddenly a strong earthquake shook the jail to its foundations. The doors opened, and the chains fell from all the prisoners.

When the jailer woke up and saw that the doors were open, he thought that the prisoners had escaped. He pulled out his sword and was about to kill himself.
(Acts 16:19–27)

Insights

Great story, eh? It's very hard to get to grips with the realities of this story, for a couple of reasons. The first reason is that you're probably reading this book while you're in your living room with a nice drink and a biscuit, or you're tucked up in bed, or maybe sitting on a cosy, warm train. Another reason is that, once we know how the story ends, we have a happy, triumphant feeling the whole time we're reading it. So what I'm going to ask you to do is to try as hard as possible to forget the end of the story. Forget that there's a massive earthquake, which causes everyone's chains to fall off, and forget the wicked jailer getting into a state and wanting to kill himself. Also, if you can, forget your surroundings – the central heating, the half-eaten biscuit oozing with chocolate and caramel, the fluffy duvet. . .

Now imagine yourself not just in prison, but in the inner

prison of a prison (the inner prison was right in the depths of the building and would have been very small and claustrophobic). Not only this, but your feet are chained to heavy blocks of wood and your body is lacerated with deep wounds from a whip. Your clothes have been torn from you, it's cold, and you have no idea what's going to happen. As far as you know, you could be spending the rest of your days there. That's the situation. So what do you do? Well, I'll tell you what Paul and Silas did: they sang songs of praise to God. That's honestly what they did.

Painful praise. That's what this chapter's about, because that's what life is sometimes about. There are times when the most painful things happen, and what's required of us – before we do anything else – is that we praise God.

The reason for this is that in our sorry natural state we sometimes think we're worshipping God, but really we're just worshipping our circumstances, happy that life is going so well. Nothing is really required of us in this kind of situation, as there's no necessity for depth in our walk with God when there are no trials. We say that we love God regardless, but actually there's no way of knowing that until a few things get stripped away. That's what happened here, and there are plenty of other examples through the Bible and through history. Let me give you one example.

In the Bible there was a man called Job, who had everything, including a great relationship with God. In a matter of a few days, though, he lost pretty much everything, including all his children. All he had left was his wife, and God, who obviously seemed very distant. His response? He tore his clothes and shaved his head (a sign of mourning), and then fell to the ground and worshipped, saying, 'Naked I came from my mother's womb, and naked I shall return there. The LORD gave and the LORD has taken away. Blessed be the name of the LORD' (Job 1:20–21 NASB). That's true worship and it was Job's greatest moment.

It's not that God enjoys seeing us suffer; it's just that we very easily become reliant upon things like comfort and ease to the point where, in our hearts, these things can replace God. Because of this, and because of God's commitment to making sure we're the real thing and not fakes, He will at times let things happen which reveal what we're *really* like. These moments are massive opportunities to grow in God. They're perfect moments to demonstrate the reality of all those songs we've sung. Without these moments we're in danger of thinking that we mean certain things that we actually don't. This is the beauty of trials.

Coming out of all this, I want to encourage you to develop the habit of praising God in all kinds of situations. When life is really inconvenient, before you start moaning, start praising. When you meet someone really annoying, instead of immediately giving them an earful, give thanks. When *nothing* is working out as you would like, instead of throwing up your hands in exasperation, throw up your hands in praise. Don't do this because you feel like it; do it because God is worthy of it. He's worthy when things are going great, and He's worthy when things are going terribly.

We sometimes make the mistake of thinking that our priorities, plans and preferences are the same as God's, but do you know what? God is about a lot more than making life convenient for you and me, and the sooner we realise this, the easier it becomes to roll with the bumps and scratches of life, and even laugh and sing when it doesn't go quite as we'd hoped. God is under no obligation to make life easy for us – life in all its fullness is about a lot more than that!

The Bible describes praise and worship as an offering and, at times, as a sacrifice; and as you probably know, a sacrifice always involves death. There are certain things that we have to die to if we're going to live fully for God – but it's always worth it!

Look at Paul and Silas, singing away! Can you imagine the other prisoners sitting there in their cells listening to the songs of truth, love and joy? They probably can't believe their ears! The only songs ever heard before in that place would have been the songs of drunkards or mockers, but suddenly the praises of God are filling the place. Paul and Silas are not ashamed, and neither are they discouraged. This is apostolic Christianity and it's both beautiful and powerful.

And look at God's response. You get the impression that God was so bowled over by their love for Him that He just had to 'do' an earthquake! What else can you do? I suppose it makes sense, if you're God, just to explode with delight over these two gospel soldiers. That hidden, dark, impenetrable prison gets shaken to the core by the glory and power of God – and what caused it? Painful praise. Although this was a literal earthquake, we need to realise that painful praise has the potential to release spiritual 'earthquake' power from God into all kinds of situations, so that chains fall off people and dark places get shaken by the radiant presence of God.

We need such a big picture of God. I heard of a man who had been stuck up a tree for days as a result of torrential rain and floods where he lived. I think he was up there for about three days. Can you imagine that? He'd probably got no sleep during that time, and would have been cold and hungry.

When help arrived, his first response was to praise God for His goodness! His chief concern wasn't how God could have let him remain stranded up there for three whole days. No – he was just bowled over at the mercy of God in rescuing him. That's the difference between someone who's self-important and someone who has understood that they're an object of mercy. One is never contented and the other lives gratefully, no matter what. Which will you be? If you're a Christian, then the answer shouldn't be a difficult one.

I'll finish with the words of the psalmist (Psalm 150):

> Shout praises to the LORD! Praise God in his temple.
>   Praise him in heaven, his mighty fortress.
> Praise our God!
>   His deeds are wonderful, too marvellous to describe.
> Praise God with trumpets and all kinds of harps.
> Praise him with tambourines and dancing,
>   with stringed instruments and woodwinds.
> Praise God with cymbals, with clashing cymbals.
> Let every living creature praise the LORD.
>   Shout praises to the LORD!

The result

Just before the jailer kills himself, Paul stops him and explains that all the prisoners are still there! The jailer checks, and he's so amazed that he falls down before Paul and Silas and asks what he must do in order to be saved. He and his family become Christians and get baptised that very night. He also takes Paul and Silas out of the cell and bathes their wounds. They get released the next morning and carry on travelling around preaching. Amazing!

Conclusion

Paul and Silas made the most of a difficult situation by worshipping and seeking the Lord. They didn't allow themselves to lose heart or take their eyes off the King, but instead brought to mind all that was true about God and used it to praise His name. This was worship at its highest point, when everything else was stripped away. Your troubles may be less dramatic, but if you use them to the glory of God, who knows how many 'earthquakes' you'll experience!

Ask yourself

- Will you throw up your hands in worship before you throw up your hands in exasperation?
- How will you follow King David's advice and not let yourself forget all the benefits of knowing God (see Psalm 103:2)?

14

The Martyrs Cry Out
for Judgement

Setting the scene

Because the scene I'm about to describe takes place in the
book of Revelation, I hope you'll have sympathy with me
when I explain that, in all honesty, I'm not sure what on earth's
going on! No, that's a slight exaggeration, but hopefully you
know what I'm getting at – we're being let in on heaven, and
mysteries abound. We'll pick up the narrative as some seals on
a scroll are being broken, which symbolise the righteous
judgements of God on the earth. The seven seals symbolise
God's perfect and complete judgement (the number seven in
the Bible usually symbolises completeness/perfection). Let's
pick it up as the fifth seal gets broken.

> *And when He broke the fifth seal, I saw underneath the altar the*
> *souls of those who had been killed because of the Word of God,*
> *and because of the testimony which they had maintained; and*
> *they cried out with a loud voice saying, 'Master, You are holy and*

faithful! How long will it be before You judge and punish the people of the earth who killed us?' And there was given to each of them a white robe; and they were told that they should rest for a little while longer, until the full number of their fellow servants and brothers who were due to be killed as they were should be brought in.[1]

Insights

Before I start here, let me just admit that this isn't an easy subject. I've included it in the book, though, because I think it would be cowardly not to.

Let's just get this straight. We're getting a glimpse of the throne room of God, and those who are crying out to Him are the souls of the martyrs. A martyr is someone who has been killed specifically for their faith in Jesus. It's also worth noting that they're not told off for asking how long they have to wait before they see God's judgement come on their killers. God doesn't say, 'Call yourselves Christians? How could you say such a thing? I really expected more of you!' No. All that's said is that they're to wait a little while longer.

One of the reasons why this is so tricky is that if you think back to Chapter 11 (the chapter on forgiveness), Jesus really nails the fact that all Christians need to forgive completely those who have wronged them if they're to enjoy a close walk with God. And yet here we have a group of martyrs (who surely had a close walk with God), in God's presence (where no sin can remain), asking Him to hurry up and stretch out His hand *in judgement*!

---

[1] Revelation 6:9–11, author's own translation.

What's going on here? What's going on is that throughout the Bible you often meet with teachings that seem to oppose one another, but that need to be held together at the same time without getting your knickers in a twist (if you'll pardon the expression!), and here's a fine example. There are plenty more examples like this and, if we handle them well, we end up with a mature and full expression of godliness. It's when people overemphasise one particular thing that they often get into trouble and heresy.

God is a judge; in fact God is *the Judge*. It's an intrinsic part of His nature, and it's utterly wonderful. Because He's the Judge, we can rest assured that every wrong will be put right, whether now or on the day of eternity. This is actually one of the reasons why we can forgive people who hurt us, because we can rest assured that one way or the other, the sin committed will not go unchecked. There will indeed be a day when all those who are dead, the great and the small, will stand before the throne and be judged for the deeds they did while on the earth (see Revelation 20:12). There's no getting away from this, and being a Christian does *not* mean that you try to forget this. In fact, in Romans 12:19 Paul urges the Christians in Rome not to take revenge on those who have wronged them, but instead . . . do what? Forgive them? Well, yes, but that's not quite how Paul puts it here. Paul says don't take revenge, but 'leave room for the wrath of God' (Romans 12:19 NASB). Paul is saying that you're not to worry about those who wrong you, because God will certainly deal with them – in wrath, if they don't repent.

So how does this work with forgiveness? I think it works like this. When people wrong you, you let it go, and you ask God to bless them and bring them to repentance, that they might experience the same mercy that you have. Within that, you also ask that if they won't repent, God might deal with them in righteous judgement. This way, you feel absolutely no responsibility in terms of getting them back. I want to make it clear here that the emphasis should definitely be on praying for their forgiveness and blessing. In the Romans passage we looked at a minute ago, Paul ends by saying, 'Do not be overcome by evil, but overcome evil with good' (Romans 12:21 NASB). I'm definitely not encouraging you to ask God to punish people and to go into great detail about what you want Him to do to them! What I'm saying is that we can be confident that God will deal appropriately and wisely with those who have wronged us, and we can ask Him to do so with a clear conscience. John Stott writes:

> Evil men should be the object simultaneously of our love and our hatred . . . to love them is ardently to desire that they will repent and believe, and so be saved. To hate them is to desire with equal ardour that, if they stubbornly refuse to repent and believe, they will incur God's judgement . . . it is a natural expression of our belief in God, that He is the God both of salvation and of judgement, and that we desire His perfect will to be done.[2]

I do think it's significant that the martyrs pray this prayer while they're in God's throne room. In that place there's no room for sin. What they're asking is coming out of a righteous desire to see justice done on the earth, not out of bitterness or resentment or anything of that nature. It's ever so important that we make sure we don't use 'judgement prayers' to mask hatred

---

[2] John R. W. Stott, *The Message of the Sermon on the Mount*, IVP 1984, page 117.

and bitterness, because Jesus is clear that we're to love our enemies and bless those who curse us.

Having said all that, sometimes things happen in life that are just terrible. Unthinkably disgusting things are done on our planet and in our lifetime. Thankfully, we *normally* only ever hear about them on the news; it's rare that we experience such things directly. However, when we do experience these things, the kinds of emotions we go through are horrendous. It's not simplistic and easy to get over; these things can cut really deep. In these situations we need to know a few things. First, that the person/people who did it is/are still within reach of the same gospel mercy that came to us. Second, that we don't have to hold on to the anger and bitterness, but can release them to God, knowing that He can bring healing. Finally, that if there's no repentance from those who did this, there will be a day when the terrible wrath of God will right-eously fall on them for all to see.

It's OK to say this to God, and it's OK to be relieved that He will put all things straight. Isn't He amazing?

The result

Some Christian-killers (like Saul, who became the apostle Paul) get saved and wonderfully transformed by the gospel. Others don't. Those who don't will be dealt with thoroughly by God, but this won't happen until the proper time, when all those who are to be martyred have been so, and those who have lived righteously have done so, and those who have lived wickedly have done so. The end will come and justice will be done.

Conclusion

We are to be those who are confident in God. We should always pray primarily for mercy and grace, knowing that if God doesn't act in this way, He will surely act in judgement. Because of the cross, where God's mercy met God's justice, we can pray confidently for the salvation of our enemies, knowing that the price has been paid, but knowing also that God is certainly no 'easy touch', and that if repentance isn't forthcoming, judgement is just around the corner.

Ask yourself

- Will you forgive, desiring the best for everyone – even those who have hurt either you or someone you love?
- Will you trust in the righteous judgements of God and forsake revenge, leaving room for His wrath?

15

John Longs for Jesus
to Come Again

Setting the scene

It's the last-but-one verse of the whole Bible. The apostle John
has just been receiving an amazing revelation of the glory of
God, the risen Lord Jesus, the victorious church, the titanic
struggle of good against evil, the return of Christ, the Day of
Judgement and the new heavens and the new earth. He's
understandably awestruck:

> He who testifies to these things [Jesus] says, 'Yes, I am coming
> quickly.' Amen. Come, Lord Jesus.
> (Revelation 22:20 NASB)

Insights

John was the disciple who seemed to be the closest to Jesus
when He was on the earth. He appears to be the one
described as the disciple whom Jesus loved (see John 13:23;

9:26; 21:7). Now, we know that Jesus loves everyone, so what was meant by that term? It probably meant that there was a special bond of affection between the two of them, like you get with best mates. They would have been close. We read in the Gospels that during the Last Supper, as Jesus was reclining at the table (in that part of the world you didn't sit at the dinner table, but lay down around it), John was also lying down, but was leaning his head on Jesus' chest (see John 13:23). There was certainly no religious formality here.

However, at the beginning of the book of Revelation, John sees his best friend Jesus again, but this time, instead of leaning on Him and chatting, he falls down on his face like a dead man (see Revelation 1:12–17). The reason for this is that he's face to face with the *glorified* Jesus.

When Jesus came to earth, He emptied Himself and became just like us, and only every now and then (like on the mount of transfiguration – Mark 9) would His true glory be seen. Because of this, from a physical point of view, there was nothing remarkable about Jesus. This all changed after He rose from the dead and returned to heaven. In this amazing vision of Jesus that John has in Revelation, he sees Him as He is – awesome. The result is that he's utterly overwhelmed. Jesus has to reassure him that it's OK and he has nothing to fear (see Revelation 1:17).

For the next 21 chapters, the glory of Christ is beautifully revealed. He's shown to be the Lamb of God who was killed for the sin of the whole world, and who overcame sin, death and Satan (see Revelation 5). He's seen as the only One worthy to open the scroll of God's righteous judgements (Revelation 5). He's seen as the mighty warrior who wages war with the nations of the earth, and the One who has all authority as

King of kings and Lord of lords (Revelation 19). He's seen ·
the One who's right bang in the middle of every local church,
rewarding here, rebuking there, intimately involved in every
aspect of church life (Revelation 2 and 3). He's seen in the centre of God's throne (Revelation 5), as well as leading out the
armies of heaven on a white horse (Revelation 19). He's
altogether lovely.

The point here is that John goes from being like a dead man
in chapter 1 to saying these simple words full of desire in
chapter 22. As the wonder of Jesus is unfolded before his
eyes, he regains the old affections of the Last Supper, but
mixed now with a reverence and awe that perhaps were never
there before. His feelings are summed up in one word:
'Come.' He just wants Jesus. He just longs for Jesus. That's the
conclusion of the Bible; that's the result of having a genuine
heaven-sent experience of God – more love for Jesus. You
can't graduate or move on from that. That's the pinnacle of
Christian experience – longing for Jesus' presence. That's
what Christian maturity looks like – desire for Jesus. Simple,
isn't it?

A Christian author once wrote this: 'The value of a soul can
only be measured by the object of its love.' This means that to
find out the measure of someone, you need to look at what it
is they love the most. If you can find out their passion, you can
assess what kind of person they are. John's passion was Jesus.
His chief concern was to meet Him on that final day and be
forever joined to Him in never-ending intimacy. That says a lot
about John. What's your passion? What's the object of your
love? Money? Church? Ministry? Girl/boyfriend? Peer group?
Music? Be brave enough to ask yourself.

Look at your prayer life to see whether you're more

ncerned with the blessings Jesus brings or with Jesus Himself. Don't be afraid to put the spotlight on yourself; it's better to find out now, while there's time to reorder things, than later, when there isn't.

The Bible teaches that all things were made *by* Jesus and *for* Jesus (see Colossians 1:16). That's profound. That not only tells you *how* you came into existence, but it also tells you *why*. This is the reason for your existence: Jesus.

Now bear in mind that this glorious King has affections for you that are hard to measure. His love for you led Him to the cruel cross, where He took on your wicked master (sin) and the enemy of your soul (Satan) and came out victorious. His love for you burns as strongly today as it ever has, because He is 'Jesus Christ . . . the same yesterday, today and for ever' (Hebrews 13:8). Not only this, but He is also determined to teach you how to love Him. This is why He has given you the Holy Spirit.

The Holy Spirit will teach you how to pray (see Romans 8:26; 1 Corinthians 14:2), will help you understand the Bible (see John 14:26; 1 Corinthians 2:13), will help you grasp all that God has done for you (see 1 Corinthians 2:12), will give you gifts (see Romans 12; 1 Corinthians 12; Ephesians 4), will lead you into truth (see John 16:13), will help you (see John 16:7), and will fill you with all power and boldness (see Acts 1:8; 4:8–12), but, more importantly than anything, He will reveal more of Jesus to you (see John 16:14–15; Ephesians 1:17; 3:14–19).

The Bible is clear that we only love Jesus because He first loved us (see 1 John 4:10, 19). See His love for you. Feast on it. Take time to gaze on Him in all His loveliness. The result will be love for Jesus.

The result

Jesus will respond to that cry to 'Come' when not just one or two of His people say it, but when the bride is prepared for the groom. Think about it. What motivates a bride to get prepared? Love for the groom. That makes all the difference. When that heartfelt cry goes up from the church, the result will be that Jesus comes.

Conclusion

John was bowled over with a vision of the risen Jesus. As all His lovely attributes were laid out before him, his response was, 'Come, Lord Jesus.' As we use the love and desire we have for Jesus to fuel greater love and desire, more and more often we'll find that our hearts are saying 'Come, Lord Jesus' as the things of this life grow increasingly dull.

Ask yourself

- What do you prize above all else, really?
- How will you make time to gaze on the risen Lord Jesus, feasting on His love for you and cultivating a desire for Him?

Another One of Those Moments

I suppose it will be just like any other day. We'll all be doing the kinds of things we normally do. Then, just like that, it will all be different. It will be the moment that changes everything. A trumpet will blast and will be heard around the globe at exactly the same moment (see 1 Corinthians 15:52). And that will be it.

It will be the dawning of a new age; an age where, for those who know Christ, there will be no more tears, or sickness, or suffering. God Himself will say, 'See, I'm making everything new.' There will be new heavens and a new earth. We will have new bodies. Everything will be new (see Revelation 21:3–5).

All that we knew about God, by faith, will be confirmed before our eyes. We'll see Him face to face (see Revelation 22:4), and in an instant we'll become like Him (see 1 John 3:2). We'll honestly be in the fullness of God's presence for all eternity, never to be taken away. It's too glorious to imagine.

On that day we'll be rewarded according to all that we've done in our lives (see 1 Corinthians 3:10–15). The criterion for ccess won't be busyness or 'worldly' success, but obedience (see Matthew 7:21). We'll understand fully that all God required of us was to do what He asked us to do. We'll see at that moment that the most important aspect of our existence was that we were in communication with God; nothing fancy, just conscious, deliberate, soft-hearted communication (see Hebrews 3:15; 4:7).

Well, that moment hasn't come yet, and we find ourselves in an age of imperfection. The world we live in is anything but new. The battle is fierce – it's an age of warfare for us. We would all rather it wasn't, but we can't pretend. Because of this, we must take up our armour (see Ephesians 6:10–20) and for the love of God and the glory of His Son, we must fight the good fight of the faith (see 1 Timothy 1:18; 6:12). But keep your ear to the ground: you never quite know when He's going to appear (see Matthew 24:36)!

That's the end of the book, but for you, I hope, it's the beginning of fresh adventures into God. Go for it.

Survivor Music

Let the Rain Come: Newday Live 2007
The 2007 Newfrontiers' Newday event saw over 6,000 young people coming together from all over the UK. Matt Redman joins Newfrontiers worship leaders Simon Brading and Paul Oakley for inspiring times of worship, featuring a host of new songs to resource the church.

Going Your Way: Simon Brading
Simon Brading is the worship leader for Newfrontiers growing national youth event Newday and the Newfrontiers student and twenties event Mobilise. Simon is crafting worship songs that are the voice of a new generation of worshippers. Including You Reign and I'm Alive.

Facedown CD & DVD: Matt Redman
Facedown worship always begins as a posture of the heart. It's a person so desperate for the increase of Christ that they find themselves decreasing to the ground in an act of reverent submission. Featuring the songs Worthy, You are Worthy and Nothing But The Blood. The DVD is nearly 4 hours long and contains all of the songs on the CD plus The Heart of Worship, 3 messages from Louie Giglio, 'Global worship conversations' with, Darleene Zschech, Graham Kendrick and 'Notes on songwriting' with Matt Redman and Tim Hughes.

Beautiful News: Matt Redman
Beautiful News offers another excellent collection of modern anthems for the church. Includes songs written with Beth Redman (You Never Let Go, Fearfully and Wonderfully Made), Paul Baloche (Greater Song) and Martin Smith (Take it to the Streets). Matt has managed to shift his creativity into a brand-new gear. Beautiful News is full of energy, excitement, mission and movement.

www.survivor.co.uk

Survivor Books...receive as you read

Incomparable: Andrew Wilson
God Most High. The Lord. I Am. YHWH. Father of our Lord Jesus Christ. Maker of heaven and earth. There can be no greater inspiration, no more solid ground for hope, no other reason for worship, and no stronger motivation to live well. Andrew explores 60 names and descriptions of the one true God, weaving profound biblical insight into each chapter, and so unfolding the greatest subject we can ever contemplate.

Conspiracy of the Insignificant: Patrick Regan with Liza Hoeksma
Patrick Regan grew up in a nice, quiet, middle-class Christian family. So he got something of a culture shock at 16 when he spent two weeks doing a mission in London. Having met people from violent backgrounds and living in cardboard boxes with no food, money or security, Patrick prayed a life-changing prayer: that he would see things the way God sees them.

Worship, Evangelism, Justice: Mike Pilavachi & Liza Hoeksma
We know that worship is much more than singing songs to God. Don't we? This book looks at what happens when we let Worship infuse all areas of our lives, what Evangelism looks like in today's culture, and what God's passion for Justice means in a broken and hurting world.

Eden: Called to the Streets: Matt Wilson
Something is happening in our cities. A quiet miracle. Followers of Jesus are moving out of their comfort zones and planting their homes and their souls in urban community. They choose to live out their lives in the face of some of the highest rates of crime, social deprivation and drug and alcohol abuse. Matt Wilson tracks this amazing story of Eden in Manchester, from early beginnings in the 1990s to the brink of a whole new generation of disciples on the streets.

www.survivor.co.uk

The Shock of Your Life: Adrian Holloway
Dan, Becky and Emma have one thing in common...they just died. Were they ready ? The Shock of Your Life is a book that will change your life. This award winning book has altered peoples ideas of what really happens when we die. The question of whether there really is a heaven and hell is answered here.

Aftershock: Adrian Holloway
Dan is back. Back from the dead. Now there'll be trouble. Dan was the sole survivor of an accident that propelled three young people into the afterlife. Now he's back, ready to convince his friends and family that Jesus is their only hope before they face judgement after death. Adrian Holloway gives readers and youth leaders a powerful weapon in their spiritual armoury.

Facedown: Matt Redman
When we face up to the glory of God, we soon find ourselves facedown in worship. When it comes to expressing our worship, what we do on the outside is a reflection of what's taking place on the inside. Matt Redman takes us on a journey into wonder, reverence and mystery - urging us to recover the "otherness" of God in our worship.

www.survivor.co.uk

God on the Beach: Michael Voland

Newquay: the UK's infamous summer party capital. The town heaving with young clubbers and surfers, each one desperate to live life to the full, eager for experience, ready to ride the waves and hit the heights. Into this chaotic carnival dropped Michael Volland, dj, surfer, and team member in a beach mission 21st century style. There was just one problem, Michael was not at all sure that God would turn up.

God on the Road: Andy Frost

Join thirteen ordinary twenty-somethings as they head for the sights, sounds and smells of Europe. They're drawn by the surf and the night life, but something else has brought them here, something that makes this road trip a pilgrimage. Armed only with a pocket phrasebook and the gospel, they soon find themselves in the company of the heroes of history. And they find that Jesus is already on the road ahead of them.

Red Moon Rising: Pete Greig

24-7 is at the centre of a prayer revival across the globe and this book gives a fantastic insight into what God is doing with ordinary prayer warriors. Brilliantly written with pace and poetry, this gutsy true story of the rise of the 24-7 Prayer movement is peppered with miracles and hard times of suffering. Read inspiring stories of people finding a new depth of heartfelt prayer and radical compassion.

God on Mute: Pete Greig

Writing out of the pain of his wife's fight for her life but also the wonder of watching the prayer movement they founded touch many lives, Pete Greig wrestles with the dark side of prayer and emerges with a hard-won message of hope, comfort and profound biblical insight for all who suffer in silence. Tracking Christ's own unanswered prayer through Gethsemane and Golgotha, the book leads the reader to Easter Sunday where miracles arise – often when we least expect it.

www.survivor.co.uk